Backyard Bones

Also by Donna and Patricia DeMuth

*   *   *

In a Little Town Called Paxton

Is burning down the garage really the best way to enliven a boring Saturday afternoon? Is it possible to cut your contributions to the church by 75% without incurring divine retribution? How do you reinstate rationality when military thinking goes out of control? Can you effectively dispose of a bucket of dirty scrub water by throwing it out the window? Can you ban puberty? Most importantly, how do you do all of this when you are under the age of twelve? Find all the answers and much more in a little town called Paxton.

A closely-knit family living in a small, rural community during the 1950's and '60's provides the setting for this delightful collection of stories. With gentle humor, the authors take you along as they revisit their childhood and share some of the trials and joys of growing up. By the time you turn the last page, you will be eagerly looking forward to another visit.

*   *   *

Merry Christmas From a Little Town Called Paxton

What can possibly stop a determined six-year-old from visiting Santa? Did Dad go shopping in the Twilight Zone for the new Christmas tree? Could a Christmas miracle really have happened in Paxton, Illinois? Did Guinness agree about the world's tallest Christmas tree? Is an Audubon Guide a needed tool when decorating Christmas cookies?

Playing The Ghosts of Christmas Past, Donna and Pat take us back, once again, to their childhood home and memories of Christmas to find answers to these questions. Told with the authors' quiet humor and trademark wry twists, these stories will both charm and entertain you. *Merry Christmas from a Little Town Called Paxton* is an eagerly awaited and most welcomed sequel to *In a Little Town Called Paxton*.

Backyard Bones

Donna R. DeMuth
and
Patricia J. DeMuth

iUniverse, Inc.
New York Lincoln Shanghai

Backyard Bones

iUniverse books may be ordered through booksellers or by contacting:

iUniverse
2021 Pine Lake Road, Suite 100
Lincoln, NE 68512
www.iuniverse.com
1-800-Authors (1-800-288-4677)

ISBN: 978-0-595-45069-5 (pbk)
ISBN: 978-0-595-89380-5 (ebk)

Printed in the United States of America

This book is dedicated to our brothers, Jim and Ray DeMuth. With one of you on either side of us, you formed the bookends of our lives. Thank you, guys, we love you both.

Contents

Acknowledgments

Over the course of writing three books we have learned that books are not created in a vacuum. Many people are involved, either directly or indirectly, in the creation and success of a book and we would like to thank them.

First of all, a huge thank you goes to all of the people who have purchased, read and shared our first two books. Each book sold is a confirmation to us that we are on the right track, and the positive feedback that we get from our readers is like a dose of ambrosia. Your continued encouragement and enthusiasm is the fuel that keeps us going.

Others are more directly involved in the final product. Once again, Shawn Bean did a tremendous job of editing for us. His gentle and humorous corrections are astute and welcome, and go a long way toward polishing the final product.

Another thank you goes to Kathleen Reavey Lee, the artist who created the picture on the front cover of this book. After we outlined our idea to her, she spent some time prowling in the cemetery and peering through evergreen hedges to capture the feel of our old backyard. Those impressions, coupled with her wonderful imagination and talent, gave us a book cover that was all we could ask for. As it turns out, Kathleen's work is also featured on the cover of *Merry Christmas From a Little Town Called Paxton*. She had done the drawing of the Paxton town Christmas tree and contributed it to a project sponsored by PRIDE of Paxton. PRIDE gave us permission to use the drawing, and we are now delighted to finally attribute that drawing to Kathleen and to thank her for both of the book covers.

We can't forget Carl Hudson, Jr. who has been an enthusiastic supporter of our work since the beginning. Carl has carried our books in his store, Hudson's Drug and Hallmark in Paxton, since *In a Little Town Called Paxton* was published in September of 2004. He graciously allowed us to scramble the traffic in his store with book signings and has "kept the faith" now for over two years. Carl retired at the beginning of this year and his son, Andy Hudson, is now continuing the support. All in all, Carl, Andy, and the members of their staff have been responsible for selling several hundred copies of our books, and we offer a heartfelt "thank you" to all of them.

Another thanks to the other merchants in the area who are also carrying our books, most notably Pages For All Ages in Savoy, Barnes and Noble in Champaign, and Market Street General Store in Paxton. We deeply appreciate the support and exposure, and our hope is that you will be rewarded with ever increasing sales.

A nod and a round of applause go to Frank Drendel and Mary Sue Dietrich for their enthusiastic response and support, which are deeply appreciated. We'll do everything we can to move these books further into the public eye.

Finally, we want to recognize the members of our family who have been so encouraging, patient and supportive throughout this process. Thank you Ray, Shelly, Kevin, Shawn, Angel, Caressa, and Jody for everything you have done in helping us to achieve our dream.

Some Background ...

"I don't believe that these stories are true, not at all."

Donna and I looked up to see a rather stout lady planted firmly in front of our table, clutching her large purse to her chest like a shield. We were doing a book signing and up until then the day had gone fine.

Donna replied, "Excuse me?"

"These books, these stories." The woman waved her arm over our table to clearly indicate exactly which books she was talking about. "They simply cannot be true."

Donna tried again. "Have you read them?"

"Yes, I have, both of them."

"Well, I'm sorry that you didn't enjoy the ..."

"I didn't say that. The books are very amusing, and some of the stories are quite funny, but it's obvious that they are not true."

I had finally gotten far enough past the initial shell shock to be coherent again. I looked at the woman and asked, "Why would you say that?"

"Why, it's obvious. You have quoted conversations in them, and the level of detail is amazing. You couldn't possibly remember all of that. After all, you were just *children* when these things supposedly happened, and that's all I wanted to say." She turned on her heel and strode away from our table.

I looked at Donna and muttered, "What the hell was that all about?"

Donna grinned back at me and said, "Our number-one-fan, maybe?"

We turned our attention back to what was going on around us, and finished the day without any other strange incidents occurring. On the drive back home we were both fairly quiet, mulling over the day. It had been a very successful book signing and we were basking in the glow of the positive feedback we had received from readers. However, the lady who thought we were liars was still rumbling around in my brain and stomping on my sensibilities. I glanced over at Donna and said, "After all, we were just *children* ..."

Donna shook her head and said, "Could you believe that? It completely broadsided me. I can't imagine what set her off."

"I'm glad you kept enough composure to be able to answer her—I was speechless for a minute or so."

"You can't win them all, and you'll go crazy if you try."

*　　　　*　　　　*

Looking back on it, this incident occurred around the time that another literary contretemps was in the news. Oprah Winfrey had featured an autobiography in her book club and, upon deeper research, it was discovered that portions of that book were not as true as they had been represented. This had set off a storm of controversy about veracity in books, and apparently had also set off the lady who questioned our books.

Hanging on the wall above our computer workstation is a picture by the artist Debbie Lamb. It is a charming picture of a country house and landscape, and it bears the inscription "Home is where your story begins." We keep the picture where it is as both an inspiration and a reminder—home truly is where our stories begin.

While we were growing up, our parents strongly encouraged the development of the arts of communication. Reading, writing, and verbal skills were all given a high level of respect, and conversation was an important part of our lives. A good example of this was that every evening we all sat down together for a family meal, and during the meal the television or radio was turned off. Dinner was not simply a way to feed physical hunger—Mom and Dad made sure that our brains were fed and exercised as well. Over the meal, we discussed our day and what had happened—in other words, we shared the stories of our lives. As we grew up, this emphasis honed our memories and our skills for sharing those memories with others. Several of the stories were so good that they were repeated many times over the years, usually prefaced with "Remember when …"

With regard to the stories in our books, the core of each story is true and each tale is based on something that actually happened. Are these stories verbatim accounts of what happened? No. Though we have stayed as close to the truth as memory allows, they are stories. Quotation marks are used to indicate conversation. We knew the people well enough that we can assure you that the words credited to individuals could well be what they would have said, and we have done our best to keep the spirit and the personalities as true as we can. As far as the details about our home and our town, all we can say is that we grew up there. Paxton is a small town, and each of us explored it and memorized it from end to end as we grew.

Most of the stories in our books are "the good ones" that we have repeated and shared with friends and family many times over the years. Through use, they have become as familiar and as comfortable as an old pair of slippers. Through repetition, the details have stayed fresh in our minds. We have put them into writing to keep them from being lost and to share them with a wider audience. Our hope is that you enjoy them as much as we do.

That brings us to the book that you are now holding and reading—*Backyard Bones*. We have found that writing a book is, in some ways, very similar to raising a child. You start out with a goal, and plans and ideas of guidance to reach that goal. But books, like children, can soon develop their own personalities and introduce changes and turns that the "parents" never envisioned. The question then becomes do you force it back to plan, or do you allow it to grow and flower on its own with what guidance you can provide?

When we began this book, we had a plan and an outline for a book of stories about events that our Dad always described as "This is great. It should be educational for the kids." Each event did teach us things, though usually not quite in the way Dad had in mind. As the pages began to fill with words, however, we discovered that we had a bright but wayward child on our hands—the stories kept drifting away from the outline. After several discussions and a few bouts of writer's block we decided to go with the flow and see what flowered.

We ended up with a potpourri of stories that cover the transition from childhood into adolescence with the attendant learning, growing and stumbling that we all do at that time. One of the stories involves real bones in the backyard, a few others touch on the cemetery (our extended backyard), and a few of them are skeleton-in-the-closet stories that up until now have been shared with a very limited circle of family and friends. Since Mom and Dad didn't have a lot of closet space for skeletons, we decided those stories qualified as "backyard bones" as well. Once again, these are all essentially true stories, though in some instances we deliberately changed some names to avoid any possible embarrassment. We hope you enjoy them.

"This makes as much sense as a soup sandwich."

—Ex-husband who will
remain anonymous

Words Can Be Deceiving

… as told by Donna

One sunny summer afternoon, Jim and I were out in the backyard "practicing" our golf swings. (Jim was twelve and I was ten.) We were using Dad's grass tool that he used to trim around trees, bushes and the fence. It made a fairly good substitute for a golf club.

In our household it was understood that everything had a purpose, and a tool was not a toy. Dad had impressed on us that using tools incorrectly could result in injury or breaking the tool.

Well, we certainly weren't using the grass tool for what it was designed for and, sure enough, we broke it! It just snapped in half when Jim made a spectacular long shot to the mulberry bush (the fourth green).

We were also taught that, when you mess up, you 'fess up. We didn't try to hide the deed, because it was just a matter of time before Mom and Dad uncovered the truth. So, when Dad got home from work, we confessed sorrowfully, and promised to never do it again. Dad reminded us (again) that his tools were not toys, and that since we broke it, we were responsible for replacing it, using our own money. He informed us it would cost about $2.00, and we could buy one at the local Coast-to-Coast store.

Now I have to interrupt here, and explain something. My father was a "lifer" in the Air Force. Everything in his world was substituted with acronyms (like AWOL), idioms, or military appellations. Little did we know (in our innocence) that many of the words we routinely used were not the common names of those items.

Every now and again, when a young airman needed an extra lesson in discipline, he was assigned to cut the grass on the parade field using that particular tool. Dad had just sent us to the Coast-to-Coast store to buy an *idiot stick*.

1

*   *   *

We hopped on our bikes and headed downtown. Jim had $2.25 and I had 88 cents, more than enough to cover our purchase. Of course, my brother pointed out to me that it was supposed to be half-and-half, so I would owe him the difference for my half if that ran more than 88 cents. (I still believe he would have made a great CPA or banker.)

Jim reminded me that Mr. Robinson, the owner, wouldn't put up with kids messing around in his store, so we would have to be in there and out as quickly as possible—and to let Jim do all the talking. Most of the kids in town never ventured into the Coast-to-Coast without a parent. Mr. Robinson had a *reputation*—supposedly he hated children. He readily met any unaccompanied kid(s) just inside the front door and eagerly chased them out. It was years later that I realized that he was a very congenial man. He just had too many items in that store that kids could harm themselves with, and the little imps made him nervous.

When we entered the Coast-to-Coast Mr. Robinson, who was behind the counter, greeted us with a demanding, "What do you kids want?" In a very business like voice Jim responded with, "We would like to buy an idiot stick, sir." I backed Jim up with what I thought was a winning, friendly smile. We were totally unprepared for Mr. Robinson's reaction. After being told in no uncertain words that we were "not funny, that if we didn't have anything better to do with our time, he did, and he did not have Prince Albert in a can," we were quickly and unceremoniously ushered out of the store.

Jim and I stood outside on the sidewalk thoroughly dumbfounded. All I could say was "Who's Prince Albert?" Jim said "never mind," and then decided that Mr. Robinson had misunderstood us, or maybe thought that we didn't have any money. We went back into the store to clear up any misunderstanding. The second time around we were told, "to get out and if we came back again, he would call the police and our parents!" Wow! A double whammy! Now we were totally bewildered, especially since there was an idiot stick displayed in the far corner of the front window.

We didn't know what to do. I voted to go back home and tell Dad that the Coast-to-Coast store was temporarily out of idiot sticks. Jim voted to try one more time. We walked back into the store, and before Mr. Robinson could say anything, Jim announced that we would gladly buy the idiot stick in the window. That time, Mr. Robinson actually started to come out from behind the counter. We fled in terror.

We were stymied. The only answer we could come up with was to call Dad and explain to him what was going on. We pushed our bikes down the sidewalk to Davis' drugstore, where Dad bought our Sunday paper and we spent our weekly allowances. Mr. Davis was always in a good mood, and he knew us. Maybe he would let us use his phone.

Mr. Davis happily allowed us to use his store telephone. We called home and haltingly tried to explain to Dad our dilemma. He listened patiently and silently, until Jim had finished telling our sad story. The silence extended for several seconds. Then Dad said, "You idiots. An idiot stick isn't called an idiot stick, it's called a grass whip!"

"What!" was Jim's reply. I was tugging at his sleeve, trying to figure out what was going on. He covered the mouthpiece with his hand, and leaned over towards me.

"It's one of those Air Force words," he loudly whispered.

"What is?"

"Idiot stick."

"What's it really called?" I asked.

Before he answered my question, Jim said goodbye to Dad, and hung up the phone. "It's really called a grass whip."

"Oh, no." I lamented. Dad had done it to us again.

"No wonder Mr. Robinson thought that we were playing a game on him. I'm not going back in that store and embarrass myself. Sometimes I wonder, deep down inside, if Dad doesn't secretly hate us."

"He doesn't hate us. He's just too used to *Air Force Talk.*"

Back to the Coast-of-Coast store we went, red faced and stuttering. We tried to explain to him our error, and politely asked him to please sell us a grass whip. Mr. Robinson sold us one ASAP from the supply he had in the back of the store (we didn't have to buy the one in the display window), and wished us a good day. He was obviously relieved to get us little idiots out of his store.

"Where is your sense of propriety?"

—Bernice DeMuth

Bringing In the Sheaves

… as told by Pat

"A tapeworm," I announced. "My brother has a tapeworm and nobody cares."

Jim glanced at me from across the table, rolled his eyes and helped himself to another two pieces of toast, liberally spreading them with a thick layer of homemade strawberry jam. He had already consumed a bowl of cereal, a large glass of milk, and two other pieces of toast with jam. At age fifteen, he was well into the teenage male syndrome of continual food consumption.

I nudged Donna and asked, "What do you think? It's gotta be a tapeworm, right? No one normal can eat that much and stay that skinny."

Donna, who was thirteen and into dieting, gave her grapefruit a push and said, "All I know is that it's not fair."

At the end of the table, Mom sipped her coffee and said, "No one has a tapeworm, and that's a poor conversation subject at the breakfast table. Patty, you mind your own meal and leave your brother in peace."

I sighed and went back to my bowl of Cheerios, trying to think of something to do that day. Before I had formulated a plan, Mom started talking again.

"I want to do some canning today. The beans have come in very well and need to be picked. So, right after breakfast, I need you kids to go out and pick them for me."

"Gosh, Mom, I was going to clean the living room today," answered Donna. "Yesterday I noticed that the bookcase was a little dusty, and I thought I'd vacuum for you." As nutty as it seemed, she would volunteer for anything to avoid working in the garden. Donna did not get along well with dirt and bugs.

5

"Thank you, Dear, that would be nice. I guess Jim and Patty can pick the beans while you do that. Right after you get done with breakfast, you two, all right?"

Jim nodded his assent, too busy chewing to talk. My mind raced as I tried to find a reason to get out of bean picking. I didn't mind the dirt or bugs, but our garden had been known occasionally to harbor snakes and I *did* object to them. Assuming a casual air I said, "Our garden sure grows a lot of stuff, and the veggies really get big—bigger than what you see in the grocery store."

Mom agreed. "It does produce very well, doesn't it? We're lucky to have it. It gives us fresh food all summer, and enough to can so we have free vegetables for almost the entire winter."

"You know what? I saw a movie last year—Jim and Donna saw it, too—about these grasshoppers, you know? The grasshoppers ate some *huge* tomatoes that had gotten radiation on them, that's why they were so big. And then the grasshoppers got huge, too, from the radiation, and then they went crazy and started eating everything. That happened right around here. Paxton was in the movie."

"I think I remember that movie," Mom added cautiously, waiting to see where this was all going.

"Well, I was thinking about that." I paused for a second, to heighten the dramatic impact of what came next. "I think maybe our garden got some radiation on it, too, and that's why everything out there gets so big. It's probably dangerous to eat it, or even to touch it."

Jim had quit eating and was now grinning at me from across the table. Mom glanced at the ceiling with a suffering look, took another sip of coffee, and then looked me straight in the eyes. "I think," she said, "that you have a remarkable imagination. However, our garden's production has more to do with good soil, good compost, and good climate than with radiation. You and Jim are going to pick the beans for me, I'll can them, and in good time we'll eat them and just take our chances with the side effects." She stood up and carried her coffee cup to the kitchen.

Jim was chuckling as he said, "Nice try, Twerp. Weird, but nice try. How about if you pick the green beans and I'll get the wax beans?"

Donna added, "You know, Patty, that was even dumber than your usual dumb stuff. Everyone knows that movie was make believe, and Mom wouldn't fall for it."

"Yeah? Well, at least I don't have to spend the morning cleaning the living room. Talk about dumb!"

"And I don't have to spend the morning out in the garden with the snakes—the big, slithery corn snakes."

I shuddered at the thought. The three of us quickly cleared the table and stacked the dirty dishes in the kitchen sink. Donna went to get the vacuum cleaner while Jim and I went to the basement and collected two baskets. We carried the baskets upstairs and went out the back door.

As Jim and I started for the garden, I ventured a question, "Uh-h-h, Jim? Do you think the snakes are out in the garden?"

"There might be one or two. Just leave them alone."

"Do you think it'll be the corn snakes? They're awfully big."

"Just leave them alone. They're more scared of you than you are of them. As soon as they're aware of you, they'll take off."

"But, what if they don't? What do you do if one attacks you?"

Jim stopped and looked down at me. "As much racket as you make, you'll scare any snake in the world away. But if you see one, even if it's an anaconda, just stand still and holler at me. I'll come chase it away. Okay?"

We started off again. I had to hurry to keep up with Jim's long-legged strides. "Uh-h-h, hey, Jim? What's an anaconda?"

"They're big, they're ugly, and they live in South America, not Illinois. That's all you need to know about them right now. Now, stop fussing and let's get busy."

We had reached the edge of the garden. Jim moved off to the rows of wax beans and started picking. I stared down at the thick green vegetation spread out in front of me. Tentatively, I raked my foot across the top of the bean plants within reach, watching carefully for any reaction. Nothing. I peered across the garden, looking for any suspicious movement among the plants that might indicate the presence of a snake. Nothing. Apparently, the snakes had the day off and weren't going to give me a chance to get hysterical and get out of the chore. With a sigh, I moved into the first row of green beans and started picking.

The thing about picking anything in the garden was that it was boring. The garden was over an acre in size, and Mom and Dad always planted lots of everything. Picking meant moving up down the *long* rows, doing the same thing over and over. To alleviate the boredom, I would imagine myself in different situations as I picked. Once, I imagined that I had found the delta of a gold-bearing river, and there were lumps of gold just lying about to be collected. I set speed records for picking with that fantasy, but it killed my back.

This year I had a new interest. In school we had learned a little about the Civil War, slavery, and the Underground Railroad. There was actually an old mansion in town with a secret tunnel that had been a stop on the Underground Railroad. According to legend, many slaves fleeing north had been sheltered and assisted in our hometown. Fascinated by the subject, I had gone to the library. I checked out *Gone With the Wind, Uncle Tom's Cabin*, and a book about Negro spirituals. I had finished reading these shortly before summer, and (mistakenly) believed myself well educated on the topic.

As I started picking the beans the boredom set in. It was time for an alternate reality that was more fun. I decided that I was a slave on an old Southern plantation. I imagined a blazing sun driving the temperature up to about a hundred degrees, with accompanying ninety-nine percent humidity. I had been in the fields since daybreak, and exhaustion was taking its toll. Under the demands of the heat and the backbreaking labor, I slowed to a crawl as I moved down the first row of beans, dragging my basket behind me. Soon, I was singing mournful spirituals to keep myself going. I don't know how long I was at this, but it seemed only a short time when I heard a loud "Harrumph!" behind me.

I straightened up slowly, stretching my back and shading my eyes from the relentless sun. Using my forearm, I wiped the imaginary sweat from my tortured brow. Jim was standing behind me. "Patty! *What* are you doing?" He sounded very exasperated.

I cast my eyes down, scuffed a shoe in the dirt and replied, "I'se pickin' dese heah beans."

"Well, you couldn't prove it by me," he retorted. "For Heaven's sake, I'm almost done and you're barely into your second row!"

Wearily, I looked up at him and said, "There's a pow'rful lot of dese beans, and it be awful hot t'day."

He snorted, "It is *not*—it's only about seventy degrees out here. And why are you talking like that? What's the matter with you, anyway? Let me see—how many beans have you picked?" He yanked my basket closer to him and peered down at the thin layer of beans in the bottom. Then he looked at my "completed" row of beans. In a voice of utter frustration he continued, "For God's sake, Twerp! You've missed half of them! You're going to have to do that row again, and you better do it right. C'mon, wake up and get busy!"

In terror of the lash, I cringed back and answered, "Yassuh, Massuh Simon, suh! I get right to it. I be pickin' dese beans." I yanked a few beans off the nearest plant to show my good intentions.

Jim threw his hands up in disgust and stomped off. I started over on the first row of beans, this time making sure I was getting them all. I did move faster, but I was soon back in the midst of my fantasy.

When I was about halfway down the second row of beans, I heard Jim shout at me, "I'm done. I'm taking my beans up to the house. Hurry up, Twerp." I waved a languid hand at him, secretly delighted that the cruel overseer was leaving the scene.

As I was finishing the second row of beans, I was still the abused, overworked slave. I was singing *Swing Low, Sweet Chariot* for inspiration, and I was putting a lot of emotion into it. When I reached the end of the row, I stood up, closed my eyes and threw my head back, belting out, "Comin' for to carry me ho-o-o-o-me." A flourish of my arm accompanied "A ba-a-nd of angels comin' after me-e-e ..." I opened my eyes and found myself face to face with my mother. She was standing at the edge of the garden, arms crossed over her chest, looking at me as if I had just crawled out from under a rock. Jim had ratted on me.

"Uh ..., um-m-m ... Hi, Mom," I stammered.

"Patricia Jean! What do you think you are doing?"

I glanced around me, then proffered my basket and said, "Picking beans."

"Taking forever to do it, I notice. But I was questioning the dramatics. Exactly what were you doing?"

"Oh, *that*," I said. "I was just singing to myself to help pass the time."

She gave me a penetrating look that told me she knew that wasn't the half of it. Then she sighed heavily, and said, "I want you to listen to me carefully, because I am not going to repeat myself. Slavery was a shameful institution that should have never been allowed to exist. It's an unfortunate part of our history, but any *thinking* person is glad that it was abolished. Also, a person is a person, no matter what color their skin happens to be. They are no different than you. I simply cannot believe that a child of mine would be so insensitive as to make a game of it. Furthermore, that phony drawl is insulting." Then came the zinger—"*Where is your sense of propriety, young lady?*"

I hung my head and said, "I'm sorry, Mom. I was just pretending ..."

"Well, you can pretend something more suitable. And if you want to sing to make the job less burdensome, try *Oh, Susanna!* or *She'll Be Comin' Around the Mountain*. If you pick beans to that beat, you *might* get done sometime before sunset!" She turned on her heel and strode back towards the house.

Abashed, I set myself to finishing as quickly as I could and carried my basket of beans back to house. I spent the rest of the morning helping Mom with the canning. I washed and snapped beans for her, and got a practical lesson in food preservation. We sterilized jars, filled them, and used the big pressure cooker to seal them. Mom explained everything to me as we worked. It was interesting, and it was sort of fun, but in the back of my mind I mulled over Mom's words at the edge of the garden.

The lesson sunk home, and that was the last time I was an overworked slave. When it came time to knock the tomato worms off the plants, I was a fighter pilot machine-gunning enemy snipers out of the trees.

"There are some days when something sweet helps everyone. Have a piece of chocolate."

—Bernice DeMuth

Dracula Has Risen, Again and Again and Again

… as told by Donna

I had just gotten home from catechism on Saturday morning. Mom was in the kitchen fixing lunch. Since it was Saturday, and Dad was home, lunch was more substantial than a quick tuna or bologna sandwich. We were having hot dogs with buns, pork and beans, cheese and macaroni, and sliced tomatoes and cucumbers.

I went directly to the kitchen and started snooping in the pans on the stove and generally checking over the menu.

"Hello, honey, how was catechism today?" Mom asked, as she turned from the sink, checking to ascertain if I was messing in her prepared food.

"It was okay. Boy, am I hungry!"

"Get your fingers out of the macaroni, Donna. You can wait a few minutes more until we sit down to eat."

"What did you learn this morning?" Mom asked, trying to take my mind away from the macaroni.

I had to remove my finger from my mouth, to answer her. "We learned about the seven deadly sins, and all that."

"What!" she asked, slightly surprised.

"Yeah. I don't remember all of them, but they are the worst sins you can commit. Things like greed; eating too much at one time, like at Thanksgiving; and vanity, which I don't really understand; and lust."

"Lust!"

"Yeah, like wanting something really, really bad, that you're not supposed to want."

"Oh," she said, and got busy again slicing the cucumbers.

I watched her intently, wondering how she could slice them so evenly.

"Hey, Mom, can I go to the movies with Gail tonight? She said if Dad will take us, her dad will pick us up. The movie's at seven. I gotta call her and let her know."

"What's at the movie?"

"Oh, it's a scary movie called *Dracula*. Kind of like *Godzilla* or *Rodan* or something like that."

"Why do you want to see a scary movie?"

"They're really fun. The monsters don't even look real, and we make fun of them, and laugh and boo at them."

"That's kind of silly, isn't it?" she asked, looking at me quizzically.

"I guess. But that's what we do. Lots of the other kids are going."

"Did you check the movie on the acceptable list posted at church?"

"Yup. Gail and I checked after catechism. It's on the "B" list." (The Catholic Church was way ahead of the times, and had already established a censor list for movies. A "B" rating meant it was acceptable for children, with parental approval.) I poked my finger into the macaroni and cheese again.

Without a word, or even a glance, Mom lightly smacked the back of my hand with a wooden salad spoon she was using.

"Ouch!" I yelped.

"Keep your fingers out of the food, Donna! Now, go wash your hands, and then set the table for lunch."

"You hurt me!"

"I did not hurt you, and you know it. Get along and set the table."

"What about the movie?"

"I guess it's all right to go to the movies, if your Dad agrees. Do you have enough money?" (If a child wanted to go to a movie, they were expected to plan for that expense out of their allowance or other moneys they had saved. Parents just didn't hand over loose change at random.)

"Yup. Thanks, Mom, I'll go ask Dad."

Before she could catch me, I skipped out of the kitchen and went looking for my father. I can't honestly say who set the table for lunch, but I know it wasn't me.

*   *   *

I had the necessary twenty cents to get into the movie—plus, the additional fifteen cents needed for a Slo-Poke caramel sucker bar. Boy, did I like those things! They lasted through an entire movie, made your tongue raw, and your jaws hurt, but you knew you had gotten your fifteen cents worth!

The theater wasn't packed with kids like it normally was on a Saturday night. We had our pick of seats: two-thirds of the way down and exactly in the center of the row. That way we made sure we wouldn't miss a thing.

Even at the tender age of twelve, I was a movie buff. I knew all the current actors and actresses. When I could afford it, I would buy popular movie magazines. I would cut out the pictures of the movie stars, and paste them in one of my homemade scrapbooks. I would thumb through the pages, making up stories for the stars to act out. I was already on my way to becoming a storyteller.

After checking to see whom else was in the theater, waving at other friends, and giggling about the boys, Gail and I settled down to watch the movie.

It didn't start out like the other scary movies I had seen. The music was dark and the movie was gloomy. It made me a little uncomfortable right from the beginning. I thought that maybe it would get funnier as the story went on.

There was this guy who stopped in this old village to ask the way to Dracula's castle, and to see if he could get a ride. The people in the tavern he stopped at weren't very nice to him, and refused to give him any help, and kept making the sign-of-the-cross every time he brought up Dracula's name. All they would agree to do was take him as far as the crossroads outside of town. He had to walk the rest of the way; it was almost dark and cold and windy. Wolves were howling in the background. If I had been him, I would have waited until the next day, and then walked to the castle in the sunshine!

(As the years passed, I quickly learned that the heroes in vampire movies would always go off to hunt the vampire(s) at night. They also split up or went alone. Didn't make sense then, and it doesn't make sense now.)

Anyway, when he got to this really creepy castle, the main huge door just opened on its own. He went inside, but no one was there. He walked over to a big table in the main room, put down his things and took off his coat. When he turned around this pretty woman, who looked like she was wearing her nightgown, was standing in the doorway of the room. She ran up to the guy saying she needed help because the Count was keeping her in the castle against her will. She pleaded with him to save her from the Count. She threw her arms around his neck and cried on his shoulder. He just stood there holding her and telling her that he would try to help her. All of a sudden she opened her mouth, grew these long, pointed fangs, and tried to *bite his neck!* Oh my God, she was a monster! (I had never seen a vampire movie before; in fact, I wasn't even familiar with vampires and didn't know exactly what they were.)

Then Dracula appeared at the top of the stairs, looking like a huge batman in a cape. He roared/growled/shouted at the woman to leave the guy alone because the guy was *his!* Dracula had nasty long fangs too!

Whoa, Nelly! That was more than I could handle. This definitely was not going to be like a Godzilla movie, and I didn't want to see any more! My jacket, which I had taken off and was holding in my lap, quickly went over my head and the Slo-Poke. I peeked out the side of my jacket to see what Gail was doing. She was sitting next to me with her sweater over her head.

I couldn't look. I didn't want to look! I waited several moments, and then whispered to Gail, "Are you looking?"

"N-n-nope" she said in a small voice.

"I'll look, if you'll look." I bargained.

"N-n-nope."

This exchange went on for about ten minutes. Neither of us would come out from under our covers. Finally, I couldn't really hear anything bad coming from the screen, so I told Gail, in a muffled voice, that I was ready to "look." She said "Okay," but did not agree to join me.

I slowly lowered my coat so I could see. Geez Louise! To my horror, there was Dracula, full faced on the entire screen, fangs exposed and dripping with blood! Bad timing on my part! Back under my coat I went.

Not to belabor the point, it seemed that every time I got up the courage to "look," the same thing happened again. There he was, fangs and all, filling the screen. I had given up on Gail—I had enough trouble just trying to get my own timing down. (You probably wonder why we didn't leave the movie and go outside and wait for Gail's dad. What? Go outside and wait in the *dark?* Are you *nuts?)*

When the movie was over, I'm sure we were both in a state of shock. There was no talking about it, no giggling, and no sarcasm. It didn't even help that, at the end of the movie, the hero killed Dracula. I don't think it was a convincing enough finale.

We quietly went outside and found Gail's dad waiting for us. We drove home in complete silence. When we got to my house, I said "'nite" to Gail, thanked her dad for the ride and quickly scampered up our front steps and into the house. My folks were sitting in the living room watching TV. "How was the movie, Sweetheart?" Mom asked.

For a moment I gave her a blank stare. "Oh, I guess it was all right. Kind of dumb. I'm going to my room now."

She gave me a puzzled look. "Okay. Goodnight, then."

*   *   *

All I can say is that *Dracula* was one nasty movie, and I was too young to see it at that time. My calm, innocent life had been greatly intruded upon. It took months, even years, to get over the concept of vampires. To make matters worse, we lived on the edge of town and our back property line met the town cemetery's east edge. Before my "Dracula" experience, the cemetery had been a quiet, serene locale where we kids would ride our bikes on the paths around the well-manicured lawns, practice our reading from the headstones, and admire the beautiful flowers on the various plots. After the movie, it became a place of suspicion and dread. I would eye those small mausoleums with a great deal of fear, knowing that they had to be little houses for vampires!

I must admit that, for weeks after I saw *Dracula*, I couldn't sleep peacefully at night by myself. Humiliatingly, I bugged my little sister to share her bed with me. I made her sleep on the outside edge of the bed and I took the side against the wall. That way, if a vampire got into the house, she would be the most convenient victim. To make life even more miserable, I made her close all the windows at night (it was the middle of the summer, and we did not have air conditioning), look under the beds, and check the closet. This went on until one day my Mother took me aside and forbade me to continue harassing my sister. (The little blabber mouth!)

The movie pointed out that if you slept with a cross around your neck, Dracula (or any vampire) couldn't bite you. Well, I reasoned that more was better, and slept with *nine crosses* on a chain around my neck. I was lucky I didn't strangle myself during the night.

When my Mother confronted me about my strange behavior, I broke down and told her about the gross movie I had gone to. She gave me some comforting words, but also reminded me that she had warned me about seeing those kinds of movies. She reassured me that there were no such things as vampires, and that no one was going to creep into the house at night and bite me on the neck. I wasn't convinced! And, in spite of Mom's words, I slept with the crosses for months and months, and I avoided the cemetery like a plague.

When Jim, my older (brainy) brother, asked me what was wrong with me, I told him about the movie and my new aversion to vampires. He explained to me that the Hollywood version of *Dracula* was a perverted retelling of Bram Stoker's story, and that I should read the book. I would find that *Dracula* was actually a "tragic love story."

Oh yeah, just what I wanted to do—read a book that reinforced the legends of Count Dracula and vampires! No way! I can assure you that the producers of *Dracula* did not portray him as a soul tormented by lost love, and believe me, I don't think Christopher Lee ever read that book either.

*   *   *

Going to see *Dracula* at such a young age was definitely a learning experience. If I might pass some of that lesson on, I would give the following advice: if a movie starts out "dark and gloomy," your chances of it getting funnier as it goes along are slim to nothing. If your Mother advises you against the activity because it is "silly" or not a good idea, listen to her—she has wisdom on her side. If you are advised to "read the book first," do just that without any argument. Oh, and one more thing—it is not easy to eat a Slo-poke when your head is covered up by a coat.

I finally did read Bram Stoker's *Dracula*. Guess what? It is a tragic love story centered on stark right and wrong. Jim was right after all.

"You can learn a lot about the world in your own backyard."

—Bernice DeMuth

Backyard Bones

… as told by Donna

It had been a stressful day for my Dad. A few weeks earlier, the backyard started getting decidedly damp in the area around our septic tank. The situation had worsened until the ground was now squishy and we had puddles of standing water in the yard. Our annual vacation to Wisconsin was coming up in less than a week, but it was obvious that we had a potentially expensive situation that needed to be dealt with first.

As a result, Dad had spent the morning in the back yard with a gentleman who drove a very large, smelly truck. The man had parked the truck in the backyard, and then removed the top from our septic tank, which proved to be equally smelly. Using a large hose to connect the tank to the truck, the man began pumping out the tank. While that was going on, Dad and the man had been talking, and then started walking around the backyard, pointing at different areas of the yard.

When it was finally over and the man with the truck left, Dad came in the house and began talking to Mom about the problem. It seemed that we needed to extend our septic field, and this would involve digging a long trench through the backyard ending in a pit where a new septic tank could be installed. Dad could save a lot of money by digging the trench and pit first. Then, the man would come back to lay the pipe and install the new tank, and we could then cover everything back over. Since Dad still had to go to work every day, and our vacation was coming up so soon, Mom and Dad agreed that the best way to handle the situation was to hire Frenchie to do the digging.

Frenchie was a misplaced Louisiana Cajun who had drifted into town several years before and decided to stay. There were conflicting stories that either an enraged alligator or an enraged voodoo queen had been responsible for his abrupt departure from his beloved swamps. It was generally agreed, however, that whichever creature was responsible, a nasty temper had definitely been involved.

Frenchie supported himself by doing odd jobs around town. The thing about Frenchie was that he was a drunk, a dyed-in-the-wool souse, and the trick to getting a good day's work from him was to catch him when he was sober. Also, because of his addiction to variously fermented liquids, his pay was usually a combination of food and cash. That worked well for everyone and assured that Frenchie would not starve to death in a drunken stupor. Other than this one colossal bad habit, he was a genial, harmless addition to the town.

Though our parents discouraged us from hobnobbing with him, the children in town knew Frenchie as the resident expert on bad omens and evil curses. We didn't mind at all that you could never find someone who had heard the tales directly from Frenchie, who tended to be gruff with children. The stories were passed around as coming from a cousin who had a friend who knew an older kid who had heard the story from Frenchie himself. To us, that was just three additional layers of proof. The whispered tales of mysterious voodoo ceremonies and "bad ju-ju" kept us enthralled and deliciously spooked

Dad went downtown and found Frenchie, then brought him out to the house to explain the job and strike an agreement about pay. Dad used little flags to mark out the path of the new trench and the pit at the end of it, and Frenchie showed up the next morning to go to work. Mom provided his meals during the day, and Dad would supervise the completed work each afternoon when he returned home. The job progressed satisfactorily for three days, and then it was time for us to leave for Wisconsin to visit our grandparents for a week.

Arrangements were made for our neighbor, Mrs. Nelson, to feed Frenchie during our absence and Dad promised partial cash payment upon our return, depending on how much of the job had been completed.

A week later we returned, tired but relaxed and happy after our vacation. We unloaded the car and, while Mom began unpacking, Dad went out to the backyard to check the progress on the new septic field. He expected to find the trench completed and the new pit at least begun. That wasn't what he found. A few minutes later he stormed back into the house and grabbed the car keys, muttering under his breath the whole time.

"Leonard? Whatever is the matter?" asked Mom.

"Oh, for cripe's sake! The trench is only out to the cherry tree, and the tools are scattered all over the back yard. Frenchie must have gotten his hands on some money and gone on a bender!"

"But, where are you going?"

"I'm going downtown to find Frenchie, and find out what the hell is going on!" With that, Dad was out the back door and into the car. He backed out of the driveway and then, with a spray of gravel on the lane, he was gone.

About an hour later he returned, looking calmer but more troubled than when he had left. He poured himself a cup of coffee and sat down at the dining room table with Mom. We quickly gathered around also, eager to hear all the details. Dad took a sip of coffee, sighed, and said, "Bernice, we may have a problem."

Mom looked at him expectantly, her eyebrows slightly raised.

"I found Frenchie, and he refuses to come back. Apparently he uncovered some kind of bones, and all he'll say is that they aren't animal bones and it's all very bad ju-ju. What bothers me is that he won't come back, he won't take payment for the work that he's done, and he's stone-cold sober."

"Bones? What kind of bones?"

"Oh hell, it's probably a cow or something! But if he won't come back, I don't know how we're going to get that septic field done."

"Well," Mom began, "I suppose the first thing we should do is see what's out in the backyard. Let's go take a look." She stood up and started for the back door, and we kids scrambled to be right behind her. Dad followed a bit more slowly.

When we got to the trench, my brother Jim lowered himself over the edge and began searching. He quickly produced a long, straight bone with a funny kind of crook at one end. He lifted it out of the loose dirt and tossed it up into the yard. A few seconds later, a second, similar bone followed it. He looked around a bit more but didn't find any more bones. He quickly hauled himself out of the trench.

Mom was holding one bone, Dad had the other, and we crowded around close as everyone examined them.

Dad said, "These are a pretty good size. They must be some kind of animal."

"I don't know, Dear. I really can't place them …"

Jim looked up quickly. "Do you think they're a *person's* bones?"

"Well, if they are, it must be an Indian," Dad retorted.

"Possibly, but ..." Mom looked at Dad and added, "You know, I think it might be a good idea if we called the sheriff about these. If nothing else, he could probably tell us if it *is* an animal." Dad rolled his eyes at this, but gave in and agreed to call the sheriff.

Early the next morning, Dad called the sheriff and explained the situation to him. About two hours later, both the sheriff and the police chief showed up in our driveway. Mom and Dad escorted them out to the trench and, of course, we kids tagged along, not wanting to miss out on anything.

The sheriff and police chief each closely examined the bones that had turned up, and then they both got down in the trench to check the area where they had been found. As they looked, they were talking quietly to each other, but we couldn't make out what they were saying. After several minutes of searching and peering at the dirt, they both climbed back out, dusting off their hands and the slacks of their uniforms.

The sheriff began, "Well, Len, we're not quite sure just what we have here. Law enforcement around here doesn't usually involve unidentified bodies in unmarked graves."

"Don't you think this is part of an animal?" Dad asked.

The police chief responded, "To be honest, we're not really sure, but we think these may be human bones. Whatever they are, though, they sure look old."

The sheriff added, "We checked our records back for about thirty years, and we couldn't find any open cases of reported missing people. And the chief is right. This does look pretty old. If it was a crime, I'd guess that whoever committed it got hauled into a lot higher court a long time ago." The sheriff glanced heavenward as he said this.

The police chief took over again. "What we'd like you to do, Len, if it's okay with you, is to just leave this alone for a few days. There are some fellas down at the university that I'd like to call and see if they can take a look at this. They can probably tell us how old this is, and whether or not it's a person or if we're fretting over somebody's old mule. Will that work for you?"

"Oh, sure, of course. But, even if it is a person, don't you think this is an old Indian burial?"

The sheriff and police chief glanced at each other for just a second, but it was a glance that carried a lot of unspoken words. "Best to just make sure," said the sheriff. "I'll ask the professors to get in touch with you directly." With that, the two men returned to their car and left us with our speculations and guesses.

*   *   *

The following Saturday at about 10:00 in the morning there was a knock on the front door. There were two gentlemen on the front steps. They introduced themselves as professors from the University; one was an anthropologist, and the other was a historian. The anthropologist started things off by asking, "Are you the family with the bones?" The expression on his face suggested that Christmas had come early.

Mom confirmed that we were indeed, the "bone family" and invited them in. Within minutes she had them seated in the living room with Dad while she produced a large tray from the kitchen offering coffee and a tempting assortment of cookies. Since the refreshments were served on Mom's best Bavarian china dessert service, we knew these visitors were VIP's and that we were expected to display our very best manners.

While everyone sipped coffee and nibbled cookies, Dad told the professors the story of finding the bones. Since Dad could be a longwinded storyteller, they got the full, unabridged edition—starting with the septic tank overflowing, through vacation and Frenchie's desertion, to the sheriff's visit, and finally to the suggestion that we call someone from the University. When he finally wound down, the two professors had a slightly glazed look about their eyes.

The anthropologist shook himself slightly and said, "Um-m-m, yes, okay. An apparent grave in the backyard. Could we see the specimens?"

"The what?"

"The specimens. The bones that you dug up. Could we take a look at them?"

"Oh! The bones! Sure. Jim, would you go get ...?"

Since my brother Jim was already on his feet and heading for the back porch, an answer was really not required. Jim quickly returned, carrying a brown paper grocery bag that he handed to the anthropologist.

The professor opened the bag, pulled out the two bones and, after a quick glance, said, "Oh yes, definitely human." He set the bag on the floor, placed one of the bones on the coffee table next to Mom's good china, and carried the other one over to the window where the light was better. He was so involved in his study of the bone that he hadn't noticed Mom stiffen and raise an eyebrow—she wasn't sure about the propriety of a grungy old bone being placed on her highly polished coffee table, and it certainly didn't complement her china! Then, she gave a little sigh and relaxed again. Apparently, in the interests of science, she would allow it.

Meanwhile, the professor was closely examining the bone that he had. He peered at it, rubbed it a bit, scratched off a bit of clinging dirt near the end, and even sniffed at it. Finally, he turned back to us and, in his best lecture hall manner, began, "Yes. What we have here is a human femur; that's the thigh-bone. In fact, we have a pair of femurs, both the left and right. They are from an adult, but I would need to see more of the bones to determine sex and make a guess at age. You are correct that the burial is quite old. I would venture these have been in the ground perhaps a hundred years or more."

"See? I told you it was an Indian," said Dad.

"Well," continued the professor, "We really can't tell that from just this sample. Could we see the rest of them?"

"The rest of what?"

"The rest of the bones. The skeleton."

"We can show you where it is. It's still buried out back."

"Oh. You didn't excavate it?" The professor sounded disappointed.

This was too much for Mom. In a polite but slightly frosty voice she replied, "Since it appeared to us that we might have broken through a grave, we felt the proper thing to do would be to disturb it as little as possible. It seemed more respectful." Then she leveled one of her "Mother looks" at the professor.

He looked confused for a moment. After all, he was a professional grave disturber and robber, and could think of nothing more fun than "excavating" an old skeleton. After a look at Mom, however, he quickly recovered and said, "Of course. Yes. Well, perhaps we could see where the grave is?"

Dad got to his feet and started for the back door. "Sure. It's this way—out in the back yard. Just come with me."

The two professors followed him with alacrity, and we were right behind them. Mom stopped the three of us to remind us to stay out from under feet and to remain polite, and then she came with us as we all moved to the back-yard.

We stopped at the edge of the trench and peered into it as Dad pointed out exactly where the bones had been found. To our surprise, both of the professors pulled off their jackets, rolled up their sleeves, and dropped down into the trench. The anthropologist practically had his nose against the dirt of the trench wall as he brushed at it with his hand. The historian was turning over clods of dirt and examining them closely.

Soon, the anthropologist asked if he could borrow a garden trowel and a small, soft paintbrush. With those in hand, he began scraping and brushing at the walls of the trench, muttering to himself as he did so. In very short order, he had exposed a bony kneecap and the tops of leg bones on one side, while on the other side the lower portion of a pelvis stuck out from the dirt. After examining these closely, he clambered up out of the trench and brushed dirt from his hands and trousers.

"I'm sure we have a complete skeleton here. From the pelvis, I would say it was a male probably in his mid-thirties or so."

"Okay," said Dad. "But how did it get here?"

The historian now spoke up for the first time. "Well, this could be an old, family grave. On the old farms, people frequently set aside an area for family burials. It could also be a little older, perhaps a pioneer grave. As people moved west, it wasn't uncommon to have deaths on the trail—illness, accidents, and so forth. The usual procedure was to simply bury the body along the trail, and go on."

This made sense, and we all nodded in understanding.

The historian continued, "This doesn't appear to be anything recent or criminal. Murder victims are usually buried in much shallower graves—you know, get rid of the evidence as quickly as possible."

This comment earned *him* a stern "Mother-look" from Mom. He blushed to the roots of his hair, and then continued, "Now, if we could excavate this, we would be able to tell more. Possibly find some traces of clothing that would help date it, or maybe some type of grave goods if this is Indian, though I don't think so. If it *is* an old family plot, there may be some other graves right in this vicinity." He looked hopefully at Dad.

Mom said, "We didn't find any trace of fabric or clothing. Wouldn't that have just rotted away over time?"

"Well, yes, but there might be more durable things. Coins from pockets, or maybe leather boots or a belt ..."

Mom replied, "I grew up on a farm. I assure you that no farmer, or pioneer for that matter, would do anything so foolish as to *bury* a perfectly good pair of leather boots or any form of money."

"Oh! Well, yes, perhaps not ..."

Then Dad asked, "Look, does the law require this, uh, body to be exhumed?"

The anthropologist answered. "No. As long as the local law enforcement believes there is nothing criminal involved here, the grave can be left intact.

Excavating it would simply provide some historical information about the area. It would be a nice summer project for my grad students, and would only take a month or two to excavate this entire area." He again looked hopeful.

My manners slipped a bit as I gasped, "That would mean digging up the rhubarb patch!" (I dearly loved Mom's rhubarb pie and strawberry-rhubarb homemade jam.)

My sister added, "And the asparagus! And you'd kill the lilac bush and the cherry trees!"

"Now, girls, remember your manners," interjected Mom.

Dad was staring down the length of his little markers as he added, "I have to get this new septic field in …"

Mom settled things by saying, "I believe we will leave this grave as undisturbed as possible. Someone buried this person with the hopes that he would rest in peace. We should respect that sentiment."

The professors sighed in disappointment, then asked if they could look around the property for a bit. Since that activity didn't appear to be quite so ghoulish, Mom and Dad graciously agreed.

At that time our property had several huge, old maple trees on it. These trees seemed ancient to us. They towered above our two-story home, and if the three of us children linked hands and stretched we could just reach around the circumference of a trunk. In very short order, the professors discovered something on the maple at the end of our driveway, and became very excited. They called us over to examine their find.

High on the trunk of the tree was a scarred patch in the bark. The professors pointed out to us lines in that scarring, and if you looked closely you could make out an abstract symbol of a mule's head, somewhat distorted over time due to the tree's growth. Examining the other trees, they quickly found two more with similar scarring; one in our backyard and another by our neighbor's barn.

It was now the history professor's turn to take center stage. He began his explanation for us. "These trees are quite old, I would say well over a hundred years old. Back when this part of the country was the frontier, goods were often transported by means of trains of pack mules. One thing that was in desperately short supply and very valuable to settlers was salt. There were salt flats in the area around Detroit. In fact, now there are some very large salt mines in that area. But, back about a hundred to a hundred and fifty years ago, traders would collect salt from those flats and, using mule trains, would bring it to the frontier settlements to sell."

"At that time, this wasn't such a nice, settled part of the country, and roads were poor or non-existent. So, the traders marked their trail by using hatchets to cut these marks, these mule heads, into the trees along the way. That way, they could find their way back and forth to the salt flats by following the marked trail. That grave in the backyard might very well be a trader that died along the trail." He then hurried back to his car to collect a camera and take pictures of the marks on the trees. After he was done, the two professors assured Dad they would inform the sheriff of what they found, thanked us politely and left.

Mom and Dad decided to bury the two leg bones alongside the rest of the grave. Mom went to church and had a Mass said for the soul of the person in the grave, and Dad spent a few weeks finishing his trench and pit. By the end of the summer, the new septic field was in place, the trench had been covered, and new grass was covering the scar in the backyard.

I had learned a lot about the history of our area, and I thought it was wonderful that our property had been part of an old salt trail. I would frequently go to those old maples and search out the mule head scars. Standing with my hand against the tree trunk, I was delighted that these living sentinels connected me to people who had lived so long ago and shared the same space that I lived in.

"A lady is appropriately dressed for any occasion in a simple black dress and a string of pearls."

—Bernice DeMuth

I Could Have Danced All Night

… as told by Donna

The whole family was sitting around the dinner table. It was fairly quiet; the only sound was the clink of silverware on the plates. We were all engrossed in our meal except for our father. He was intently staring at my two-year-old little brother, Raymond, who was sitting in his high chair next to Mom.

"What is he muttering?" Dad asked.

"What, dear?" responded Mom.

"He has been sitting there muttering sounds since the beginning of dinner. I can't make out what he's saying. But it's a little irritating."

"He's singing, dear."

"Singing? What's he singing?"

Everyone had stopped eating, and was looking at my little brother and then back to Dad. It was no surprise to us—Raymond did this all the time.

"Commercials." Mom responded.

"Commercials?"

"Yes, dear. TV commercials. He likes the jingles, and sings along with them when the TV is on. He has them all memorized."

With that said, Raymond loudly broke out in song, "brusha, brusha, brusha, new Ipana toot'paste."

We could tell Dad was dumbfounded. He dropped his fork, and just sat there with his mouth open staring at Ray. Finally he said, "Does he have to do it at the dinner table?"

"He's not bothering anyone, dear. Besides, he gets most of the words right, and I believe it helps him build his vocabulary."

"Maybe we could hire him out to the commercial people," interrupted my younger sister, Patty. Everyone ignored her.

To change the subject, and to take everyone's attention away from my baby brother, who had lapsed into another jingle, Mother asked in general, "How was school today, kids? Anything interesting happen?"

We all looked at each other questioningly.

"No," said Pat.

"Not really," responded Jim.

I didn't answer, but I did shake my head "No."

"Well, it seems you have been putting in a lot time at basketball practice, Jim. Think you have a good chance to win the game on Friday night?"

Before he could answer, I interrupted, "Yeah, a lot of time practicing ... every afternoon. I'm surprised you don't have to practice on the weekends too." This was a big contention with me. My parents thought "sports" was a good mix with all his other "brainy" activities, like student council, the Speech Club, the Math Club, etc. But I suspected basketball practice was a good excuse to dump me each weekday afternoon with delivering the entire paper route we shared. It was hard to check up on him to verify all his "practices," because I was delivering all the papers! He didn't say anything to my retort; he just kind of gave me a little know-all smile, which our parents didn't notice.

Mother quickly changed the subject again. "Donna, I understand the Junior High dance is coming up soon. It will be your first formal, dress-up dance. Aren't you excited?"

This time it was my turn to drop my fork. How did she know about that dance? I hadn't said a word about it, not even to my blabber-mouth sister.

I kind of hung my head, and said in a small voice, "I'm not going."

"I'm sorry, Sweetheart, I'm not sure I understood you. Did you say you weren't going?"

"I'm going to have a stomach-ache that night."

(Another one of those confused looks crossed my Dad's face.)

"Why don't you want to go your first school dance, Honey? You can get all dressed up and join your friends in a magical evening. The first time you go to a real party is the best!"

"I just don't want to go to some silly dance!"

Before Mom could say any more, I continued and blurted out, "Besides, no one will ask me to dance! I'll be standing along the wall all by myself all night while everyone else has fun!

"I'm sure that is not true! I've seen you and Gail practicing those dances, and you are quite good. As good as any of those teens on American Bandstand!"

"Oh, Mother, you don't understand! No one will ask me to dance because I'm fat and ugly!!" (I was going through one of my "pudgy" spells at that time. Come to think of it, I still am.)

Suddenly Dad stepped in, "You are *not* fat, and you are *not* ugly. Who told you that? I have a few things to say to them!"

(You have to understand my Father. He thought he had the two most beautiful daughters born to any man, and he didn't hesitate to tell anyone who would listen.)

"Now, Leonard, I suspect Donna is exaggerating a little."

"Yeah," Patty interrupted, "I don't think Donna's fat; she's just kind of chubby."

"See!" I said loudly. "I told you!"

"Patty Jean, you are not helping matters! We are discussing this with Donna, not you."

My sister made a gesture that indicated she had zipped her mouth shut, padlocked it, and threw away the key. She received an exasperated look from my Mother.

"If you don't go to the dance, how will you know whether or not anyone will ask you to dance?" inquired my older brother.

"Jim, has a good point there," Mom agreed.

I glared at him. "I don't want to talk about the dance any more! Okay?"

But Jim wouldn't let it rest. "If I wasn't your brother, I'd ask you to dance."

"Oh, for Pete's sake. Easy for you to say, because you are my brother!" I thought to myself.

"I think that you won't sit out one dance, and will come home complaining about sore feet." Dad decreed.

This was too much for me. I felt outnumbered and helpless to make my point. I didn't respond, and resumed hastily eating my dinner, not looking up at anyone. At least they respected my silence and dropped the subject. The rest of the meal consisted of any topic of conversation except the dance.

*   *   *

It was a full-blown conspiracy! Over the next few days everyone in the family, except my baby brother, had something to say or suggest about the upcoming dance. But, I held my ground and ignored their attempts, stoically refusing to acknowledge their efforts.

The first person to put a crack in my icy wall of silence was my mother, of course. One evening she asked me to come with her to her sewing room: she had something she needed my opinion on. This caught me a little off-guard, (Mom seldom asked for my opinion) so I readily followed. (Patty had to follow us as well—she rarely let any activity pass her by, whether invited or not).

"Donna, I wanted to show you a piece of fabric I found, and ask you what you thought about it," Mom said while retrieving some material from her sewing cabinet.

It was a generous piece of deep emerald green velvet. "Isn't it pretty," she commented, "and look here, I also found this piece of green and black brocade print that matches the velvet perfectly."

I couldn't help myself—I reached out and touched the green velvet. It was as soft as kitten fur, and the brocade had very fine threads of gold woven into the pattern. Together they shone and glittered in harmony. The cloths were just plain beautiful!

Beware! My mind warned. *She's up to something, and you are over the edge already.*

"Don't you think these two materials would make a lovely winter party dress?" Mom asked me with all sincerity.

"Yes." I whispered back in awe and wonder.

Crack! I think I actually heard my resolve splintering.

"And, look. I also found the perfect pattern to use." Mom opened her pattern box, and there in the very front was a dress pattern for a simple, but elegant party dress. I didn't know what to say.

Patty filled in the silent gap, "Black and dark colors make you look skinnier."

I had forgotten she was standing behind me. I jumped a little and turned around to find her looking at me with a big grin on her face. "I'd go to a dance if I could wear a dress like that!" she added.

"Oh, I-I-I don't know," I stammered.

"Well, think about it," Mom casually said. "I will need about a week to make the dress. Let me know if you change your mind about going to the dance." She just as casually put the pattern back in the pattern box and the material in her sewing cabinet. Out of sight, out of mind. No way!

*   *   *

Yes, you guessed it. I just could not help thinking about the dress, and how pretty it would be. I agreed to go to the dance. I also coerced my friend Gail to go with me.

The night of the dance arrived sooner than I expected. I was nervous and excited at the same time. My dress had turned out prettier than I anticipated, and Mom and Dad had sprung for the cost of a trip to Dorothy Mae's (the local hairdresser) the afternoon of the dance. That was quite a gesture on my parent's part. On our family budget, a trip to the hairdresser was very special.

When I came downstairs ready to depart, I received a wolf whistle from Dad, and a simple, but meaningful, "nice" from my older brother. My sister declared that she wouldn't mind inheriting *that dress* as a hand-me-down, while Raymond just sat on the floor, playing with his toys and quietly singing commercials. I received a soft, approving smile from my mother. Maybe the dance would be all right after all.

Not on your tintype! All that Cinderella jazz, and the handsome prince, and the fairy Godmother was a bunch of ballyhoo. I was not one of that small select group of girls whom God had made perfect, so I was not "going steady" with any one, which was the only way to guarantee you would get asked to dance. After arriving at the "winter gala" I joined all the rest of the average, slightly plump, acne-victimized, young girls lined up along the wall opposite their male counterparts. All of us were secretly hoping that some brave young man would cross the dance floor and invite us to share a waltz. *In your dreams!*

The unattached young men were too busy hooting and hollering at each other, making silly faces at the girls, trying to stand on their heads, and feigning fainting when a new song started. During the very brief pauses between songs, they made gross sounds under their armpits and/or burped as loudly as they could. They were swapping shoulder hits, wrestling and/or pretending to knock each other out. So much for my first night of magic!

*   *   *

When I got home, I acted as though I had enjoyed a great evening—my dress was the envy of all my peers, and I had my share of invitations to dance. How could I explain what had really happened to my parents, my wide-eyed little sister or my older brother?

When it came time for my beautiful, innocent daughter to go to her first dance, I kissed her goodbye and wished her a good time. When she arrived back home, I complimented her for being a good trooper, and assured her as best I could that over time things would improve.

"Damn! That's a lot bigger than it looked in the picture!"

—Leonard DeMuth

It'll Be Educational for the Kids

... as told by Pat

"I don't want anyone running off right after breakfast. Your mother and I have something we want to talk to you about."

Oh boy, another one of Dad's "announcements," this one delivered from the driver's seat of the car as we made our way home after Sunday morning church. Donna, Jim and I exchanged glances across the back seat to see if anyone looked guilty of anything. Apparently, none of us had an inkling of what was up this time. Jim rolled his eyes and shrugged his shoulders, his hands palm up in his lap. We couldn't begin to guess what it was that Dad had on his mind.

After breakfast, Dad went to his bedroom and returned to the table with several brochures in his hand. As he settled back into his chair, he laid the brochures on the table and cleared his throat portentously. "Well," he began, "your mother and I have been talking about this, and it occurred to us that we live within 150 miles of one of the great cities of America—Chicago. A city like Chicago offers some wonderful cultural and educational opportunities, and we should take more advantage of them.

"Yeah," said Jim, "like Wrigley Field and the Cubs."

"Like Marshall Field's," Donna added in a voice of reverential awe.

"Like the racetrack, you know, Sportsman's Park?" I chimed in, my eyes round with wonder at the thought of all those sleek thoroughbred horses.

Dad was silent for a few seconds as his gaze flicked between the three of us. He cleared his throat again, then said, "Actually, what we had in mind were things like the museums, the planetarium, the art gallery, the aquarium, or possibly the zoo. There are a lot of things to choose from. I have some time off coming up next week and your Mom and I thought spending a day in Chicago would be nice. We can decide together what we want to see, and we'll go during the week so we can spend the whole day and not put up with weekend crowds. So, what do you kids think about this?"

The three of us quickly agreed that it sounded like fun. After all, it was the middle of July, and a trip *anywhere* would make a nice break from the midsummer doldrums we were beginning to experience. Dad handed around the brochures, and questions and comments erupted around the table as we looked them over. Finally, after about twenty minutes, we agreed that the Field Museum of Natural History, the Museum of Science and Industry, and the Shedd Aquarium all sounded interesting. We would all be happy to go and visit any one of those, though Donna was still holding out for at least a short stop at Marshall Field's as well.

"All right, then," said Dad as he gathered up the brochures. "Mother and I will discuss this, and figure out an itinerary. We'll go this coming Thursday, so don't make any other plans for that day."

We spent the next couple of days in a state of excited anticipation about the trip. We discussed the attributes of the different attractions, and tried to guess which one Mom and Dad would decide on.

It was Tuesday evening when Dad let us know. We were eating dessert after dinner when he cleared his throat, looked around the table to be assured of his audience, and said, "All right. About the trip to Chicago on Thursday."

He checked again to make sure he had our attention, and continued, "It was really hard to make a choice between the places you want to see. Mother and I talked it over very thoroughly, and what we decided to do is this—we're going to see all three of them."

"All three?"

"Wow!"

"Isn't that kind of a lot for one day?" asked Jim.

"Well, yes, it is, but if we carefully manage our time we should be able to handle it. We'll start with the Field Museum in the morning. When we're done there, we'll have a picnic lunch before we go on to the Museum of Science and Industry. Then we'll finish off the day at the Shedd Aquarium before we come back home. How does that sound?"

"Great!"

"All right, then," continued Dad. "We'll get up bright and early Thursday morning and head for Chicago."

*   *   *

At 8:00 a.m. on Thursday, we pulled into the parking lot of the Field Museum. We were a little surprised at how empty the lot was, but Dad was delighted. "See? I told you," he said. "If you come during the week and get here early, you don't have to put up with crowds. Well, let's go."

We all got out of the car while Dad got Raymond's stroller out of the trunk and set it up. Mom first made sure that we had locked all the doors on the car and then settled Ray into his stroller. When we got to the steps of the museum, Dad and Jim picked up the stroller with Ray in it and carried it up to the doors. The doors were locked and, when we peered in through the glass, we saw that the lights were dimmed as well.

"What the hell?" growled Dad. "Why aren't they open? This isn't a holiday or anything, is it?"

"Hey, Dad!" called Jim. "Over here! This sign says that they don't open until nine o'clock, and they're open until six."

"Well, for cripe's sake! I thought for sure that they would keep government hours. Now what do we do?"

Mom replied, "Well, we wait for the hour and then continue with our day. We don't want to waste the drive to Chicago, and an hour isn't that long." She glanced at her watch. "We really don't even have to wait an hour—it's already a quarter after. Why don't we just go back to the car and wait until they open?"

Dad and Jim picked up Ray and his stroller and carried him back down the stairs, with Dad mumbling and grumbling under his breath the whole way. Back at the car, we settled down to wait. It was going to be a long forty-five minutes—it was July in Illinois, which means hot and humid. The sun was already well up in the sky, and there was scarcely a breath of breeze. Soon, we had all four car doors wide open.

Mom looked around. "It's rather warm. Is anybody thirsty?" We all agreed that we were, so she pulled out the two-gallon Thermos and the plastic picnic cups. She quickly distributed cups of tepid Kool-Aid™, and then made the mistake of asking if we were hungry. The net of it was that by five minutes to 9:00 we had demolished most of the picnic lunch that we had brought with us.

At the stroke of 9:00, we were once again standing outside the doors of the museum. The guards unlocked the big doors, and we were the first ones in the building. The guard collected our admittance fee, and then told us that Ray's stroller would not be allowed in the museum.

"But, he's just one year old and barely walking yet," Mom remonstrated. "The stroller makes it easy to handle him, and he can even nap in it."

"I'm sorry, Ma'am, but some of the strollers have wheels that mark up the floors pretty badly. It's just museum policy not to allow any of them."

"Well, do you have strollers available that don't mark the floor? We would be willing to rent one."

"No, Ma'am, like I said, I'm sorry but that's the rule. I can tag the stroller and keep it here for you, and you can pick it up again when you leave."

"Well ..."

"Ah, hell," interrupted Dad. "Raymond's not that heavy. We can just carry him, and take turns so that no one gets too tired. Go ahead and tag it." He picked Ray up and pushed the stroller towards the guard.

(I am happy to say that the Field Museum has long since abandoned this benighted policy. Today, conveyances for the young, the disabled, or the elderly are welcomed at the museum. However, this was 1957 and, apparently, the then-curator thought more of marble floors than of people.)

With all of that settled, we started to explore the museum. The African elephant tableau in the big lobby astounded us, leaving us eager and excited to see what else this magical building offered. Dad decided that it would be most efficient to be methodical, so we went up to the top floor and worked our way down, floor by floor.

As I've said before, Dad had a very military set of mind, and he delighted in schedules and itineraries. He had carefully planned the day. We were to spend from 8:00 until noon at the Field Museum. Then there was an hour allowed for lunch, followed by 1:00 to 4:00 at the Museum of Science and Industry, and ending with a quick two-hour jaunt through the Shedd Aquarium. His schedule was already in shambles, and it wasn't even 10:00 in the morning. As we walked along he was muttering to himself, trying to re-work times and places. To be fair, I don't think he fully realized the sheer *immensity* of the task he had set for himself.

For those of you not familiar with the Field Museum, it is a huge building. From the center, two long wings extend to either side, and there are three main floors of exhibits. If you add up the square footage, the display areas cover more than 350,000 square feet, and the museum staff has made the most of the space. The museum is simply chock-a-block full of fascinating items and displays.

We were walking along slowly, trying to absorb everything around us when Dad said, "Look, we need to step it up a little if we want to get everything done today." We walked a bit faster, heads swiveling from side to side, and one or another of us stopping every now and then to look at something closer. Dad spoke up again, "Now, stay together, kids. Stay with the group. If we lose one of you in here we'll never find you." He glanced at his watch. "A little quicker, too. That's it."

Dad had worked out a new schedule in his head. Since we had gotten started in the museum at about 9:30, and there were three floors, Dad figured that an hour per floor with a half hour for lunch would put us back on track. He kept hustling us along, and soon he was striding along in front, describing things to us as we passed. "Okay, over here on the left are dinosaur bones, and, up there on the right is, let's see, looks like ancient man. Keep up, keep up. Now, around this corner over here there's, um-m-m-m, there's some more old bones of some kind of animals. And over on the other wing is where the mummies are." This was delivered in his tour guide voice as we hurried through the corridors.

There were pauses for us to catch our breath and shift Ray to a new carrier. Ray was getting fussy and squirmy, and was in desperate need of a nap. Even at double time pace, it was impossible to get through the entire museum in three hours. When we finally got to the basement and the cafeteria, it was already after one o'clock. Since we had already eaten our picnic, we would eat lunch at the museum. After checking prices and a quick consultation between Mom and Dad, each of us was allowed a hot dog, a small bag of chips, and a drink.

The contents of the museum were a blur—from that trip to the Field, I only remember a few things clearly. I remember the reconstructed skeleton of a brontosaurus, and I think that's because it was just so big that it stayed in sight longer than the smaller displays. I also remember a cross-section from a California redwood with dates and events flagged on its growth rings. That impressed me because one of the events marked near the center (when the tree was young) was the birth of Jesus.

After lunch, it was on to the Museum of Science and Industry, and it was after 2:30 when we arrived there. They, at least, let us use the stroller for Ray, which was a huge relief. It's amazing how heavy a one-year-old can get when you're toting him along. It was another whirlwind tour, and again most of the displays are a hazy blur in memory. There is a coal mine in that museum and we took the mine tour, which was interesting but noisy. I also remember a huge model of the human heart that you walked through. A combination of colored lights and a recording described the flow of blood, while a loud "lub-dub, lub-dub" heartbeat echoed around you. Donna was completely grossed out by the display on embryology, and she carried on for years about how awful the "pickled babies" were.

We got back to our car at about six o'clock, and we were all tired. Dad, however, was still raring to go and the Shedd Aquarium was still on the agenda. Fortunately, when we arrived there we found that it closed at 6:00 p.m. Dad was disappointed, but the rest of us were secretly relieved. There was nothing left to do but get a quick dinner and head for home while each of us reflected quietly on our educational experience.

"The best thing about the future is that it comes one day at a time."

—Anonymous

Eastward Bound

… as told by Pat

"So," I asked my sister, "what do you think is going on with Mom and Dad?"

"What do you mean, what's going on?"

"You know—they've both been pretty quiet for the last two days, and all those long, private talks they've been having in their room with the door closed. Do you know what's up?"

"No, I don't know. They have been acting kind of strange, though."

"Do you think Jim knows?" I asked.

"Well, I don't know why he should know any more than we do," Donna replied. "Why don't you go ask him?"

"Oh, right! Like he's going to let me in his room or listen to me. I'm his *baby* sister, remember?" I paused a second and then added, "Why don't you go ask him? He *likes* you."

We were sitting on the beds in our room as we talked. Donna sighed, stood up, and said, "All right, we'll both go ask him, but he doesn't really bite, you know." She led the way out of our room with me close behind her.

Donna tapped on the door to Jim's room and asked, "Jim? Can we talk to you for a minute?"

A few seconds passed before the door opened and Jim asked, "What do you guys want?"

"We want to talk to you for a few minutes. Can we come in?"

"Yeah, come in." Jim turned and sat down at his desk as Donna and I perched on the edge of his bed. "All right, what's bugging you guys?"

I looked at Donna to see if she would lead the way, but she was looking back at me with a questioning look. I took a deep breath and said, "Well, we were wondering if you knew what was going on with Mom and Dad the last

43

couple of days. You know, why they've been acting so weird and been having all those secret discussions?"

"I haven't overheard anything specific, but if I had to guess I'd say it probably has to do with Dad's job."

I gasped. "You mean like he got fired or something?"

"No, Twerp, the military doesn't fire people. If you mess up in the military, you get court-martialed and a dishonorable discharge. Trust me, Dad would never do something bad enough for that."

"What do you mean, then? What could happen with Dad's job that would make him act so weird?" To me, Dad's job was a constant of our lives—it was always there and always the same. Sometimes the Air Force would change his shift, but when that happened he would simply go to bed early and get up before dawn so he could be to work on time. It was unthinkable that anything really bad could have happened to Dad's job.

Jim thought for a few minutes before he answered me. "I don't really know anything more than you guys do—I'm just guessing that it has to do with his job. Whatever it is, you know that Mom and Dad will let us know about it when they're ready. We just need to wait."

"But, all those long talks in their room! And they shut the door so we can't even eavesdrop! That's not fair."

Donna rolled her eyes and said, "Maybe they don't *want* you eavesdropping and that's exactly why they shut their door."

"Oh, come on. We always eavesdrop—it's part of being a kid. It's like part of our job if we want to know what's going on," I retorted.

Jim interrupted the impending argument. "Even when we overhear stuff ahead of time, you know that Mom and Dad always let us know what's going on, eventually. You two just need to stop worrying and wait patiently. They'll probably let us know by the end of the week, okay?"

Donna answered for both of us. "Okay, but, if you do find something out first, you need to let us know, all right?"

*   *   *

Our concerns were addressed the following evening after dinner. As we were eating dessert, Dad cleared his throat and said, "Well, now, your mother and I have something that we need to talk to all of you about. I'm sure you've noticed that we have had something on our minds."

The three of us glanced at each other, nodded in agreement, and focused our attention back on Dad.

He continued, "A couple of days ago I got my orders, and I've been reassigned. Your mother and I have been talking it over, trying to decide what will be the best way to deal with this, and we think we've come up with a solution that should work."

"What does that mean?" I asked. "That you've been reassigned?"

Dad took a deep breath and replied, "It means that I'm being transferred to another air base, with a minimum tour of duty of three years."

"Do you mean that we're going to have to move somewhere else in the country?" asked Donna.

"Well, yes and no—it means a move, but this is an overseas assignment," answered Dad.

"Overseas?" I echoed faintly.

"Yeah, overseas for three years," said Dad.

Silence descended over the table for a short time as our shocked brains tried to process this new and disturbing information. Even though we were a military family, we had been extremely lucky in Dad having a very stable assignment. With the exception of an eighteen-month tour of duty in Alaska during the Korean Conflict, Dad had been assigned to Chanute for over eleven years. The family had not accompanied Dad to Alaska, so for all of us children our home in Paxton, Illinois, was the only home we remembered or knew. Mom and Dad were buying the property and house, and we had just assumed that we would always live there.

Jim was the first to break the silence. "When do you have to go, Dad? And, where did they assign you?"

"They're sending me to Wheelus Air Force Base in Tripoli, Libya, and I have to leave in about two months."

"Two months?" cried Donna. "But, that's so soon! What about school, and all our friends, and the house, and ..."

"What's Libya, and where is it?" I asked. "I've never heard of it."

"And it's a minimum three-year assignment? What happens after the three years, Dad?" Jim added.

Mom now spoke up for the first time. In her usual calm, quiet tones she said, "All right, now, I want all of you to settle down. We'll answer all of your questions one at a time, calmly. We also want to know what you think about this and how you feel. I think we'll answer questions first, and after you have some information you will be better able to understand how you feel about the situation. Okay? Let's start with Jim."

"What will happen after the three years?" Jim asked.

Dad replied, "I should be reassigned back to a stateside base. The only thing that might change that or extend the assignment would be if a war started."

"Do you have any idea where you might be assigned to after this tour?" continued Jim.

"Three years from now I'll have over fifteen years in with the Air Force. Again, if nothing drastic happens, I should be allowed to request a retirement base, and I'm planning to ask for Chanute if I can."

Donna now asked, "If it's overseas, are we expected to go with you? When you had to go to Alaska we all stayed here. Could we do that again?"

Mom chose to answer her and said, "When your dad was in Alaska, that was considered combat conditions and the family wasn't allowed to accompany him. You were all very young at the time, so I don't know how much you remember about that. However, it was a very difficult situation, and those eighteen months were a very long and hard time to get through. We're in peacetime now, and we think three years is too long of a time for the family to be separated."

Dad added, "Three years is a long time. Also, even though Raymond is only three, the rest of you are old enough now to be able to appreciate living in a foreign country. It could really be educational for all of you, sort of like an adventure."

"What about school, and our friends, and everything here? Will we have to learn a foreign language to be able to go to school?" asked Donna.

"No, you would go to school on the air base over there—it would be just like going to school here in the states. There will be American teachers and other American kids from Air Force families," said Dad.

Mom added, "And you'll have the chance to meet new people and make new friends, and you can stay in touch with your friends here with letters. As far as the house goes, we've decided to keep it and rent it out while we're gone. Since there's a good chance that Dad will be assigned back to Chanute that will give us a place to live when we come back, and your friends here will still be here when we come home."

"I still want to know where Libya is," I said.

"It's in Africa, Patty," answered Dad.

"What? You mean like with monkeys and elephants and jungle and all that?" asked Donna.

Dad chuckled a little. "No, no, it's not that part of Africa. Libya is in the north of Africa, in the Sahara Desert. It's very close to Egypt."

Mom smiled and said, "Pat, why don't you get the encyclopedia out and we can look it up."

"Okay." I jumped up and went to the bookcase in the living room, returning quickly carrying the "L" volume from our set of *Compton's*. I plunked the book down on the table and started flipping through the pages, but I didn't have any luck. "I can't find it," I said. "They're sending you someplace that isn't even in the encyclopedia?"

"Are you sure you're spelling it right?" asked Mom.

"I think so. Wouldn't it be L-I-B-E-A, or maybe I-A at the end?" I flipped a page or two, but still couldn't find it.

"It ends with Y-A," said Dad. "L-I-B-Y-A, try that."

I turned several more pages to get past the "libraries" section and finally found it. There were pictures of an oasis full of palm trees, a caravan of camels, and sandstone buildings in downtown Tripoli. We discovered that during Roman times, Libya was a famous and important Roman province. In modern times, it's most important exports were dates, olives, sea salt, and hand-worked leather and metal goods. For a map, I had to get the "A" volume and look up Africa. We passed the encyclopedias around the table so everyone could share the information.

Jim then asked, "What's the time frame for all of this? You said you have to go in two months—will we go with you then?"

Again, Mom chose to answer. "Dad won't be going for two months because he has to get a physical exam and get his shot series first, and that takes about six weeks. We thought it would be best if he went ahead first by himself. That will give him time to make arrangements for somewhere for us to live while we're there. I want you kids to finish this school year here, and then we'll get our physicals and shots and such over the summer. We're going to try to plan it where we will follow Dad late in the summer or early fall. That way, you can start school at the beginning of the term over there. That will also give me time to make arrangements for renting the house, and to pack whatever furniture and such that will be shipped overseas."

"We have to get shots? I asked.

"Yes, there's a series of vaccinations that we will all have to get before we can go. Libya isn't a highly developed country and health care isn't as advanced as it is in the States. The vaccinations are for your own protection," Mom answered.

Jim quickly changed the subject by asking Dad, "What does this new assignment mean for you, Dad? Is it a promotion?"

"Yes, it is—I'll be getting my Master Sergeant's stripe out of this, and I'll get overseas pay for the three years. Also, since Libya is classified as an 'unfriendly' country and I'll be serving on a SAC base, I'll be getting hazardous duty pay as well."

"Unfriendly? Hazardous duty? What does that mean?" asked Donna.

"In the case of Tripoli," replied Dad, "it means a lucky break for me. There's a little bit of resistance to foreign influence in the country, but it's very low level. Generally speaking, Wheelus is considered a pretty safe assignment—if it wasn't, there's no way the Air Force would let dependents go over there."

We mulled all of this new information over for a bit, and found that it generated even more questions. For each new query, Mom and Dad would give us calm, rational answers if they could, and promised to find out the information for those answers they didn't have. The discussion around the table lasted for well over an hour that night. By the time we were done we found that even though the idea of moving half-way around the world was still intimidating, it was also beginning to feel like an exciting adventure.

*   *   *

The next two months passed quickly, and soon it was time for Dad to leave. We all went to the train station to see him off, and it seemed very strange to think that the next time we saw him we would be in Africa. After he left, the house seemed oddly empty, like there was a hole in it or a familiar room now missing.

Soon, however, we began receiving regular letters from Dad. Most of the letters included either photos or clippings from the base newspaper. The letters themselves were full of Dad's impressions of Libya, and Mom made a point of sharing every letter with all of us. We spent a lot of time around the dining table, discussing all the new information we were getting and the upcoming move.

Meanwhile, we were in the last month of the school term and Mom was extremely busy. She made arrangements for Mr. Baier, a local businessman, to handle the rental and maintenance of the house while we were gone. She then went through the house from top to bottom, conducting thorough closet cleanings, organizing and packing things that were going to be shipped to Tripoli, and inventorying the furnishings that were being left with the house. As the activity progressed, it felt as if we had been caught in the strong, steady current of a river carrying us inexorably to a new destination.

Finally, summer arrived. School was out, and we received our traveling schedule. The movers would come during the third week in August, and the family would leave for Tripoli during the first week of October. We were given a vaccination schedule beginning in mid-June that involved six visits, two weeks between each, to the Chanute hospital for us to get our required shots. I thought that schedule seemed excessive.

The Air Force seemed determined to inoculate us against every disease known to medical science. There were the old familiars that had to be updated: diphtheria, whooping cough, tetanus, and polio. Our smallpox vaccinations had to be "refreshed" before we could travel. Then, just for fun, they threw in things like typhus, typhoid, cholera, and bubonic plague plus some others that I don't remember. The first visit left me with five needle holes in my left arm, four in my right arm, and a very upset stomach. Mom reassured us that the first visit was the worst, and that the volume of shots would decrease with each successive visit.

She was also pretty cagey when telling us about which shots we were getting. She never hid the truth from us. Instead, she would plan the sharing of the information for a situation where escape or revolt was impossible. An example of this was when we went for our third visit to the hospital.

We were all in the car heading south on Route 45 to the air base. Since Jim had his driver-trainee license, Mom was letting him drive while she rode shotgun in the passenger seat. Donna, Ray and I were in the back seat. Mom shifted a little in her seat so that she was partially facing Jim and her voice would carry to us in the back.

"I need to let you know that one of the shots we are all getting today might make us a bit sick for a few days," she began. "I just want you all to be aware of it, and this is a normal side effect of the shot."

"Which shot is that, Mom?" asked Jim.

"Today we are getting our first plague shot. That will take a series of three shots all together, and the doctors told me they might make us ill," replied Mom calmly.

"What?" I yelped. "Plague! *The Black Death?*"

"Well, it has been called that in the past, but the proper term is bubonic plague," Mom answered quietly.

"They're sending us someplace where people have to worry about The Black Death? And, oh my God, Dad's already over there!" I gasped.

"Your father got all of his proper shots before he left, just as we are doing. And remember, these shots are for protection—better safe than sorry."

"But, Mom, we're talking about the *plague*," added Donna.

"Yes, but this is just a precaution. I'm sure they don't have carts going through the streets with people shouting *'Bring out your dead'* any more than we do. Besides, you know that plague is spread from fleas on rats and mice, and you also know that I will never tolerate vermin in our household. Oh, look, we're at the hospital now. Let's go get this over with, and I think we've had enough discussion about plague." As Jim turned off the ignition, Mom opened her door and got out of the car while motioning for all of us to follow.

As we trudged up the long sidewalk to the hospital entrance, Jim dropped back a bit so that he was walking with Donna and me. He gave me a quick, sidelong glance and then said, "You know, Twerp, you really don't have to worry that much about these plague shots—they've really perfected them."

"Really?" I asked suspiciously.

"Oh, yeah. If you want to worry about a shot, you need to worry about our *next* visit out here."

"Why's that? What are they going to do to us then?"

Very nonchalantly Jim glanced up at the hospital and then replied in a low voice, "Because that's when they give us our *leprosy* shot, and that one is still experimental."

"*What?*" I shouted, coming to an abrupt halt as he strolled on. "What did you say? Oh, no. No, that's it! I'm not going in there, they're not poking me any more, I'm not getting any more shots, and I am *not* going to Tripoli!"

Mom hurried back to me to see what was causing this tirade. "Patty! What is the matter with you? Come on, we have an appointment."

"No! I'm not going. When I get home I'm gonna call Joan and see if Mr. and Mrs. Marshall will adopt me, at least for the next three years. Mrs. Marshall likes me—I bet she'll do it."

"You are not asking anyone to adopt you, for heaven's sake! What set this off?"

"They're not giving me any experimental leprosy shot!"

"Well, who said anything about leprosy? You're letting your imagination get away from you."

"Jim did. He said next time it's a leprosy shot."

Donna and Jim had also stopped and were standing on the sidewalk with Ray a few feet away from Mom and me. Jim had a huge grin on his face.

Mom nailed him with one of her looks and asked, "James? Did you tell your sister that … Never mind, I can see that you did. You and I will talk about this later." She turned back to me and continued, "Jim was just teasing you, and the only reason he teases you so much is because he gets such a satisfying reaction out of you. Now, we are not getting shots for leprosy, and we've talked many times about why we *are* getting the other shots. Pull yourself together and come along." She took my hand and towed me the rest of the way into the hospital.

The medical corpsmen happily nailed us with our first plague shot, along with a few others. The doctors were absolutely right: after each of our three shots for plague, we all became deathly ill for four or five days. What a fun way to spend a summer!

*　　*　　*

The movers showed up as scheduled in August and took away the furnishings, trunks of clothing, and crates of kitchen goods that were being shipped to Tripoli. It left the house feeling too big and full of echoes.

Then a letter arrived from Dad saying that he had rented a three bedroom villa in Garden City, a suburb of Tripoli where a lot of American families lived. He promised to have the house all ready for us when we arrived on October 6th. Living in a villa sounded very foreign and exotic. I tried to picture what it might look like and came up with vague images of Biblical palaces.

We spent the month of September in school; Mom would not allow our education to lapse for any reason. At the end of the month, there was a small round of going away parties, and then it was October 4th and time to go. I was so excited that I hadn't slept at all the night before.

Mr. Baier picked us up at 4:30 in the morning and took us to the train station. In the pre-dawn chill, we stood huddled at the side of the tracks while the stationmaster signaled with a red lantern to stop the oncoming train. Far down the tracks we could see the headlight of the locomotive. For a few wild moments I was afraid that it wouldn't stop. I could picture the train roaring through Paxton and continuing to Chicago with our stationmaster and his lantern plastered on the front of the engine. Then there was the squeal of metal-on-metal as the brakes were applied, the train slowed and finally stopped right in front of us. The conductor helped us aboard, and we were on our way.

We spent the first day getting from Paxton to Charleston, South Carolina. The train took us to Chicago where we transferred to a plane to Atlanta. There was a layover in Atlanta, and then a second plane that took us on to Charleston. It was the first time in my life that I had been on either a train or a plane, and it all happened in the same day!

We stayed overnight in Charleston, and began our transatlantic trip early on the morning of the 5th. That trip would consume the second day with over seventeen hours in the air broken by layovers in Bermuda and the Azores. I started the day very excited, but as our big four-engine Constellation lumbered along, I quickly decided it was boring. When I peered out the window, all I could see was an unbroken stretch of water below us. As a result, I spent the day fidgeting, dozing, and pestering Mom.

The long flight combined with the time change meant that it was early morning on October 6th when we lifted off from the Azores. We still had another six or seven hours in the air before we arrived at Tripoli. I spent some time worrying about being able to make new friends and what it would be like to actually live in a foreign country. I thought about all the comfortable and familiar things that had been left behind, and felt a sharp pang of regret.

The stress of two full days of travel with little sleep began to catch up with me—I was beginning to get sleepy again. Jim woke me up to point out the Rock of Gibraltar far below us. I dutifully admired the famous landmark, then curled back into my seat and fell soundly asleep. When I next awoke, I would be in Africa and standing on the brink of an entirely new portion of my life.

"This is great! It should be really educational for the kids!"

—Leonard DeMuth

The Dark Continent

... as told by Donna

We left the Azores at 0730 Zulu Time, which I thought was appropriate since the next stop was Tripoli, Libya, on the continent of Africa. This last leg of our trip was estimated to be approximately five hours long (remember, we were flying on a MATS, prop plane), and we were expected to land some time during the early afternoon.

Pat, Jim and I were all a little nervous, excited and concerned. Mom was visibly tired and our little baby brother, Raymond, once we were up in the air, had immediately fallen asleep in Mom's lap. We three older kids had our noses pressed against the airplane's windows, trying to see anything but a vast expanse of water (the Atlantic Ocean is very, very, very big!). Jim, though, did point out the Rock of Gibraltar when we flew over it. Needless to say, we were very impressed.

The roar of the engines was so loud that it was impossible to talk to each other, so we were all wrapped up in our own thoughts. I was silently praying that this experience was going to be a worthy lesson for the family, and set us aside from our friends and neighbors back in Paxton. No one I knew had ever been to Africa nor planned to go any time soon. I also hoped that I would be able to make some new friends at Wheelus, AFB. Two and a half years was a long time to be alone.

Dad had left several months before the rest of the family, so he had time to find us a place to live while we were in Tripoli. He also had to be there to accept delivery of our household goods and personal belongings that had been shipped by freight a month and a half earlier. He assured Mother that he would have everything set up in our new house, and all we had to do was arrive safely and settle into our new home from day one. It sounded pretty good. In fact he had even bought a "new" car to use while we were there! Mom wasn't nearly as excited as we were—all she wanted was a cool room with a comfy bed on which to lie down. Aaaaah, the wisdom of age.

Finally, we could just barely make out a shoreline on the distant horizon. It was impossible to sit still! The plane was not going fast enough! There was Africa, just out the window!

We finally landed, and gathered up our hand carried items to exit the plane. We did not have to retrieve our suitcases—they were going directly to inspection. They didn't call it customs because we had landed on the air base, which was technically American ground. But our belongings still had to be checked by both American base police and Libyan officials.

After deplaning, we were directed to a nearby building that served as an airport terminal, and towards a door that was marked "Clearance." After entering that door we went through a type of customs inspection for humans. This was so different for us that all we could do was follow the line forward. The first stop was at a desk manned by a person in a Libyan military uniform who checked our passports and entry papers that Mom had all organized in this little folder. When he checked my passport, he commented to Mom, "Very pretty young woman. Very nice gold hair." Mom was taken back a little, and all she could think of to say was, "She's only fourteen."

We then had to stop at the American check-in desk and present the same papers. That guy had no compliments for anyone. He was all business, and hurried us along to the next stop.

We were directed down a hall to a room with a sign that said "Fingerprints." There we were fingerprinted and had our pictures taken for our military ID's. This was a lot more than we had expected—it was like arriving at a place where you were not trusted or wanted. Besides, it was hot—hotter than anywhere we had been yet. All the windows of the building were open, but no cooling breeze traveled through them. Raymond was getting fussy, and we were all feeling the fatigue from the very long trip. We had yet to see our father.

The last stop was in a room with a sign that read "Debriefing." (The only other time I had come across that word was in "spy" movies.) I was now certain that we were not on friendly ground. I looked around with a critical eye. There were American and Libyan military personnel *everywhere*! I scrunched up closer to my Mother, who was battling my little brother while trying to get the fingerprint goo off his little fingers before he managed to seriously smear someone. This was my first experience outside the United States in a country that was defensive and wary towards foreigners. I was about to find out how different that could be.

The debriefing room turned out to be a large area with a lot of metal folding chairs and a podium in front of a large white slide screen. As we passed through the door we were handed some booklets by a young airman, and told to find a seat. I noticed someone in the back of the room waving his arms and gesturing to us. It was Dad! Mother looked visibly relieved and rushed in his direction. The first thing she did was hand him Raymond, and then gave him a welcome hug. He appeared very glad to see us.

For the next hour or more we were lectured on what we could do and could not do in a foreign country. The booklets we were given reiterated these rules in precise, military language. I was overwhelmed. *Women, over the age of twelve, had to be accompanied by a man (father or brother for instance) when they went out in the city of Tripoli. They had to cover their hair with a scarf. They could not be dressed in slacks. They could not initiate conversation with a native man. They were to avoid eye contact with native men, etc., etc.*

Talk about being second-rate citizens! My young budding women's rights sensitivities where being chaffed raw. My older brother elbowed me, and said, "Cool it!" under his breath. "We'll talk about it later."

That "later" discussion with Jim involved a lot of comparisons, such as "It would be like walking down the street in Paxton naked" and "Women in Islamic countries are so valued by their husbands and fathers that they are offended to be seen or approached by other men, especially strangers." These comparisons were frequently interrupted by me with comments like: "that's silly, women are human too, that makes no sense, women are not objects to possess like a camel, that's a bunch of bull sh_ _!" End of conversation!

*   *   *

We had been awake since 5:30 a.m. that morning, and it was almost 4:00 p.m. when we finally exited the processing building for new arrivals. Dad had told us he would take us over to the NCO Club for an early "welcome to Tripoli" dinner, and save Mom the trouble of having to fix dinner when we got to our new villa. He had explained that everyone referred to their houses as "villas" because they all had inner courtyards and were protected from the streets. It sounded very impressive.

So far, we had seen nothing but runways and a typical military-type building. After stepping out of the front door of the terminal, we found ouselves facing sandy-like yards peppered with monkey grass, low desert shrubs, and lots of date palms. No mistaking this for the U.S.!

The sky was overcast with a thick, yellow haze, and far on the western horizon was a darker delineation line. We just stared at this image, trying to take it all in.

"The car's over there," Dad said, pointing to a parking lot directly across the street. Oh boy, we got to see our new car next! It turned out to be something else that we could just stand there and stare at—an ancient 1953 Chevy coupe! This car had more scratches and dents than it had mar-less areas. It also looked as though it had been sand-papered!

"Dad?" inquired Jim.

"It's a heavy, sound vehicle", Dad countered before anyone could say anything else. "You can't buy a *brand new* American car in Libya, for heaven sakes! We're lucky I found this one! I bought it from a young airman who was shipping back to the states, and he assured me he had performed regular maintenance on it!" The car was no longer a matter of discussion.

My mother broke the silent tension, "Well, I don't know about you, but I am starved. Let's get over to the NCO Club and find a scrap of bread or two." We all giggled a little and then piled into our "new car."

The NCO Club was closed! There was a sign on the door that announced, that because of the forecasted ghibli, the club was closed for the rest of the day. "What's a ghibli?" we asked in unison. Dad cleared his throat, and abruptly declared, "A sand storm!"

Mother hurried us back to the car, with maternal concern written all over her face. It was decided, when we were all tucked safely in our seats, that it was best to go directly home. Dad had done some minor grocery shopping the day before, and there were eggs, bacon and bread available to make a late, late breakfast. Oh well, it was better than the cold box lunches we had been served on the plane. And, besides, we were still excited about seeing more of Tripoli and our new villa.

As we exited Wheelus Air Force base and entered the land of Libya, our world did a loop-the-loop. We could not see enough, fast enough. Our heads were spinning from side to side and front to back. The realization that Paxton, Illinois lay light-years behind us slammed into our brains. We were strangers, in a strange land.

*   *   *

The road that led into Tripoli outside the base was blacktop, but only about a lane and a half wide. There were few cars on it. That doesn't mean we had no traffic to deal with. Lots of people were walking along both sides of the road. Donkey carts and camels took up the majority of the blacktop surface. There were no road signs and the traffic laws were based on one simple rule: Whoever could holler the loudest, got to go first. We did not travel over ten miles an hour, and we did a lot of stopping and going. Frequently, someone outside the car would pound on our trunk or a fender, gesture with gusto, and address us loudly, while shaking their fist at us. Dad would smile back at them and give then a friendly wave in return. Mother sat demurely on the passenger side saying "Oh, dear" and "Oh, my" over and over again. To top this off, Dad had to remember to drive on the wrong side of the road!

I was fascinated with everything around us. The women were dressed in black trousers and hijabs (long veils that totally covered their heads and faces), or in dark colored burkhas (long outer garments that covered them from head to toe, with only a small latticed opening for their eyes). The men wore loose, baggy trousers, western style long-sleeve shirts and barracans (a large outer garment similar to a roman toga that was wrapped around their waists and over their shoulders). Over time I learned that these garments had very practical purposes, especially in a ghibli such as we were about to experience. Small children were dressed in colorful, traditional little dresses, pants or caftans.

Most of the women were carrying large woven bags with food items in them, and/or large earthen jars balanced on their heads. I was impressed. I could not have taken five steps without one of those jars falling and crashing to the ground around me.

As we drove along, Dad did a running commentary on the Arab culture and way of life. I have to give him credit—he had certainly done his homework. Did you know that the camel was not an indigenous animal to Africa, and had been brought there thousands of years ago from the area that is Pakistan and India today?

When Dad paused in his information giving, Mom took advantage of the break and interrupted the train of conversation. "Is this road normally this busy?" she asked.

"No, it's not," Dad said. "Maybe it's some holiday or religious observance."

Suddenly Dad hit the brakes hard enough to knock us forward in our seats, even though we were only going about ten or fifteen miles per hours. "Don't look kids!" he decreed. We had no idea what we were not supposed to look at, but Mom seemed to have caught on immediately. "Oh, for heaven's sake!" she exclaimed. "In public!"

"What, what?" we cried in unison.

"Never mind; just keep your eyes straight ahead."

Our heads were swiveling in all directions (of course), but we didn't pick up on what had shocked our parents. Over time, this became a common incident when the whole family piled into the car for a drive. We only caught about half of the things our parents did not want us to see, but I can tell you that it was always a learning experience!

*   *   *

Mid-way between the air base and Tripoli was a small village with a very large, well-known food, produce and trade market. Dad explained that this little town was famous all over the area, and told Mom that she would probably be doing her produce shopping there. I heard her say, under her breath, "I think I'll stick with the commissary."

We crawled through the market at a snail's pace—it was thronged with people—and this gave us an opportunity to see a lot. Not to be disrespectful to the native community, but we certainly got an eye full. Remember, we children had grown up in the Midwest, and had never been exposed to anything other than what Wisconsin and Illinois had to offer.

There were no stores, and few vendors had booths or tables on which to display their goods. The majority of the products were laid out on woven mats on the ground. Small livestock were tethered to stakes, and larger animals were hobbled and tied to large posts. Chickens and fowl were kept in wooden crates. It appeared that most necessary slaughtering occurred on the spot after a choice was made (there was a lotta "don't look" directives made when we passed the animal area). The most incredible thing we saw was the abundance of flies. Everything seemed to be covered with flies! Especially if a vendor was selling meat that had already been butchered. Each merchant had a little feather fan that they frequently used to "swish" the flies away. With each swish, a small swarm of them would take flight off the meat—like a tiny swarm of locusts.

Dad explained that we were seeing an inordinate amount of goats and sheep in the market. It seems there had been a "drought" in the desert the last few years, and the herders were reducing their livestock. (I wondered how there could be a "drought" in a desert. Isn't that the point of a desert?). A lot of the vendors were already packing up their wares, even though it was fairly early in the trading day. Another indication that this was not a normal run-of-the-mill situation.

*   *   *

Our villa was located in a subdivision of Tripoli called Garden City. It all sounded so Alladin-ish. Dad explained that the city, over time, had developed ethnic out-crops. The Italians (Libya was once a colony of Italy) were in one section, the British in another, and the Americans in their area. The native Libyans were interspersed among the foreigners, as well as settled in the old part of the city. In fact, there was a cordoned off section called "The Old City" that Americans were forbidden to enter and that was taboo to all other non-natives.

At that time, Tripoli was a city almost the size of Chicago. It seemed like we drove and drove before we reached Garden City. They had an odd traffic custom that we kids thought was quite humorous. When several major roads met at one intersection, you had to go around what Dad called a "round about." This was a small, round, grassed island in the center of the intersection. You entered the area to the left, went around the little island at least once, and then merged to the right to exit onto the street you wanted. The first one of these "round abouts" we came to, Dad nervously merged into the traffic that went around the little island. The other traffic was moving as fast as it could, horns honking, drivers yelling, and fists gesturing. It was like being caught in a whirlpool. Dad couldn't seem to get an open exit lane when it came time for us to take the street we needed. We went around that silly little island about six times before we could get off the "round about." Mom pointed out that it didn't seem that efficient to her.

By the time we got to our new home, everyone was thoroughly exhausted. It was an open, airy, but well insulated house (it had fifteen-foot ceilings and the walls were three feet thick). The interior of the villa was as cool as an air-conditioned American home. We were all very relieved with Dad's choice of our new "residence."

Throughout our trip to Garden City, we had, individually and as a group, noticed the gradual change in the sky. It appeared to be getting cloudier with a yellow haze, and the air seemed to be heavier. When we pulled up in front of the house, our new "house guard," Mohammed, was awaiting us. (It was expected that American military families living outside the base needed to hire a least one house boy and a house guard. In the years we lived there, this was one of the few times we met Mohammed. The rest of the time, his "cousin" came by every Friday and collected his wages.)

Mohammed quickly helped us unload our suitcases, etc., from the car, while hurrying us along with dire warnings about the ghibli. He instructed us to immediately make sure all the windows were tightly secured, to ensure all the shutters were closed and locked, and to put rolled up blankets at the base of each door. He kept saying "very bad wind, very bad sand, Americans not like." And "sky go black and stay in house." Then he departed, leaving us on our own.

We didn't argue with him, and we followed his orders as best as we could. Dad had not experienced a ghibli since his arrival in Libya, so none of us knew *what* was coming.

We started moving our individual suitcases and various bags into our designated rooms. Mom, of course, went directly to the kitchen to check out the appliances and available foodstuffs. There was a small, but adequate, stove. Dad had put up all the pans and dishes in the cupboards, and the food was stored away on shelves or in the refrigerator. All Mom had to do was start cooking; and a good thing too, because we were starved!

Just as she took out the eggs to scramble, the electricity went out! Dad's voice boomed out of the darkness, "No one move! I know where there are two flashlights. Stay where you are until I get them."

Out of nowhere came a softly glowing light that adequately lit up the main hallway—enough light to see where you were. Mom had turned on two burners from our gas stove.

"It's a miracle," Jim said with a big smile spreading across his face.

"Well, it certainly was when it was invented," Mom interjected. We all giggled at her comment, while Dad rummaged around for his flashlights.

From that point things got worse—much worse. The wind began howling around the outside of the house. It violently rattled the closed shutters over the windows, and it beat against the large, wooden double doors in the front. We could hear "objects" hitting the outside walls and bouncing off the roof. As a group, we sought safety in the center hallway, sitting as close to each other as we could. Only my older brother, Jim, had the guts to peek out a front window through its shutter to see what was going on. He reported back that the sand was so thick and blowing so hard that he could not see two feet outside the house. It was an ominous situation we were in.

After huddling in the hallway for at least an hour, it started to dawn on us that, even though the weather was frightful, it was not affecting the interior of the house. With three-foot wide walls, the heavy front doors and the rest of our fortification, we were relatively safe. We began to relax a little.

With the aid of her miracle light, Mom managed to fix some grilled cheese sandwiches and tomato soup (she had given up on the eggs)—comfort food for her starving family.

Finally Dad decided it would be safe for us to retire for the night in our own rooms. Mom had found some candles in one of the packing boxes, and we all had some light to get ready for bed. We noticed a very fine cover of sand had settled on all the furniture—and on our bed sheets as well. We also were "breathing" this sand. It gritted on your teeth and could be felt (though not seen) on your skin. Mom said to put up with it the best we could, and we would deal with the sand in the morning.

The storm lasted all night.

*   *   *

When the ghibli was over, we had sand dunes piled up against the outside walls of the villa, and one blocking the front doors. The car was almost completed buried. The sand had to be swept away from the windows before we could pry the shutters open and let in the sunshine. One side of the patio had a mountain of sand drifted up to the roofline. (Raymond thought that was really neat, but Mom would not let him play in it.) It took us days and days to clean up the mess.

As time passed, we adjusted to our new surroundings, and even learned the tricks of dealing with a ghibli. But we never stopped missing the rolling, green farmland of central Illinois, and the richness and comfort of America.

"Santa says he's gonna find out who's naughty or nice. I like the Easter Bunny better—he doesn't make moral judgments."

—Dennis Gallagher

I'll Be Home For Christmas

... as told by Pat

Christmas was coming, but it sure didn't feel like it. It was December, 1959, and it would be our first Christmas in Libya. Up until then, being in a foreign country had been interesting and informative, but the approaching holiday emphasized just how foreign Libya was. A general depression had settled over the household, and we were all suffering from a bad attack of homesickness.

In central Illinois, Christmas meant cold, crisp weather and, possibly, snow. Homes were decorated with garlands, lights and wreaths, to say nothing of the beautiful Christmas trees glimpsed through front windows. There would be a huge town Christmas tree on Main Street, and the downtown would be festooned with lights and decorations. The stores played Christmas carols for the happy holiday shoppers greeting each other with holiday wishes as they went about their business.

In Tripoli, outside holiday displays were strongly discouraged to avoid offending the native Arab populace. The anonymous, flat fronts of the limestone villas offered little opportunity for decorations, anyway. Instead of evergreens, we had olive trees, date palms, and cactus as the predominant vegetation. Instead of snow, we had sand. Outside, the temperature was in the mid-eighties and climbing as the wind blew in fits and gusts from the south—parched, hot air coming from the Sahara and already carrying a dirty brown tinge of dust. A ghibli was coming, and by the next day we would be inundated with Hell's version of a blizzard. More than anything else, the impending sandstorm reminded us that we were seven thousand miles from home.

Mom had tried to cheer us up a bit, drawing on some of our traditional Christmas activities. She had set up the crèche set, currently containing only the manger and the ox, and had begun the month long telling of the story of the first Christmas. The Advent wreath was again the centerpiece on the dining room table, but this year the fresh greens were palm fronds rather than pine and holly. She had even pointed out that since the climate in Libya was much like that of the Holy Land, we had the opportunity of experiencing a Christmas that would be very similar to the first one. She tried hard, but it hadn't helped much.

That morning, Dad had taken the car and gone to the air base to run some errands. Mom had given him a small list of things to pick up at the commissary. Since it was Saturday, we had spent the morning cleaning house and straightening things up, but we had finished that before noon. I was sitting in the living room, bored out of my mind.

I heard the car pull up in front of the villa. This was followed by a babble of excited Arabic, punctuated by laughs, that was quickly growing louder. Curious, I got up and looked out the front window to see what was going on.

Dad had a Christmas tree tied to the roof of the car, and he had enlisted the aid of Massoud and Mohammed (our houseboy and guard) to untie it and carry it into the house. They were surrounded by a small crowd of local Arabs, all curious and talking. While I couldn't understand a word they said, it was pretty safe to assume they were discussing the foibles of those strange Americans. The discussion was punctuated by a lot of smiles, laughter, and touching the tree. Dad dispensed a few piasters of "baksheesh" as he shooed children out from under foot and led Massoud and Mohammed into the house.

They stood the tree in the front hall, leaning it against the wall. Dad gave them each a couple of piasters tip, and assured them he would invite them in to see it again once it was arranged and decorated. He walked them back to the front door, along the way collecting the five or six Arab children who had slipped inside, and guiding them all back outdoors. It was rather like trying to herd rabbits, but after a few minutes he managed to clear the hallway and close the front door.

By now, we had all gathered in the hallway also, checking out this year's Christmas tree. And what a tree it was! Dark, glistening green, it towered to a height of ten feet and the air in the hallway already carried the tang of fresh pine. We looked back at Dad in amazement.

"Well! What do you think of it?" Dad asked.

"Isn't it rather large?" Mom replied.

"Sure it is, but I figured we've got these fifteen foot high ceilings in this villa, and we might as well take advantage of them and have a really great Christmas tree. I've always wanted to have a really big tree."

"Where did you get it, Dad?" asked Donna.

"On base. Sergeant Taylor at the office told me they were expecting this shipment today. Each year, they bring in Christmas trees from Germany. He told me to just go down to the flight line today, and I could buy one right there when they unload the plane. Isn't it great?"

"But, Dear, how much did a tree this size cost?"

Dad laughed. "That's the best part of it. This baby only cost seven dollars, and that included a tip for cutting the bottom off the trunk and helping me tie it to the car!"

"I'm afraid our decorations will just be lost on a tree this size," Mom added.

"Well, the base grapevine also told me that the BX just got in a big shipment of Christmas stuff. We need some new ornaments, anyway. It's still early. I thought we'd all go out to base and do a little shopping. What d'ya say?"

Within minutes, we were all in the car and driving to the base. The BX did, indeed, have a huge selection of Christmas items, and we spent over an hour happily picking out new lights, ornaments, garlands, and tinsel. We loaded our purchases into the car and headed back home.

After dinner that evening, Dad and Jim got the Christmas tree set up in the living room. Even though it was the biggest tree we had ever had, there was still a good three or four foot clearance between its tip and the ceiling. We decided to decorate it the following day.

*   *   *

When we got up on Sunday morning, the ghibli was blowing at full force outside. We had all the shutters tightly closed, with towels tucked around windows and under doors to keep out the sand. The temperature outdoors was over a hundred degrees, but it was pleasantly cool and dim inside our villa. Dad called a quick family meeting around the dining room table.

"Well," he began, "we're not going to Mass this morning. The good Lord expects us to honor the Sabbath, but not at the expense of our lives. Driving in this storm would be suicidal. So, let's have a nice breakfast and then we can spend the day decorating the Christmas tree. How does that sound?"

We all agreed that it sounded like a good idea and promptly put the plan into action. After breakfast, Dad led the family in saying a few prayers. As soon as he was done, we all hurried into the living room.

Overnight the branches of the tree had relaxed a bit, making it appear even larger. It towered above us and filled the entire corner of the living room. Soon, we were laughing and chattering as we loaded the tree with every decoration we had. Dad had to use a stepladder to put the angel on top and to get lights and ornaments on the top four feet. When we were finished, it had five strings of lights, all of our ornaments both old and new, and several packs of tinsel. The huge tree absorbed it all without looking the least bit cluttered. It took several hours to get it all done.

Christmas carols were playing on the radio, which was always kept tuned to the air base station. Outside, the wind moaned as it found its way through the streets and between buildings. Dad turned off the lamps in the living room and plugged in the lights on the tree.

A hush fell over us as we gazed at our tree. The lights twinkled brilliantly and the ornaments and tinsel sparkled. The fresh scent of evergreen filled the villa. This was the most tremendous and beautiful Christmas tree we had ever had. It made us realize that Christmas means home and home is where you gather with loved ones, no matter where that might be on the globe.

"Oh, horsefeathers!"

—Leonard DeMuth

Just Driftin' Along With the Tumbleweeds

… as told by Donna

Jim (my older brother) was president of the Catholic Teen Club, and Dad was an adult leader. I was just a member. To celebrate the Easter season, they thought it would be neat to sponsor a trail ride for the teenagers. The Old Beach Road, which was closed, would make a nice trail. It would be peaceful and dark, and we would be able to see all the stars in the beautiful spring sky. We could build a campfire on the beach, roast hot dogs and make s'mores. It sounded good to me. I had just one small problem, but my Dad thought it could be overcome: I had never been on a horse before. He assured Mom that he would explain the techniques to me, and, after a little practice, I'd be fine. Mother appeared doubtful.

As a young man, my Father had spent several summers on my Great Uncle Bert's horse ranch in South Dakota. He was a seasoned and confident rider. Jim had worked on a Dude Ranch in Wisconsin when he was fourteen, and had also received good training on how to ride horses. They were sure that the both of them would have no trouble looking after me and helping me if I needed assistance.

In spite of Mom's warnings about chaffing and saddle sores, I was convinced I would be fine, and eagerly looked forward to my first ride on a real, live horse.

*   *   *

About twenty teenagers had signed up for the trail ride. It was a good-sized group—enough to make the event a party. Everyone was animated and talking excitedly. The whole atmosphere was electric, and I fell in with everyone else's mood.

When we had arrived at the base stables, a lot of the kids knew which horse they wanted. I guessed they had been riding several times before. I kind of hung around the sidelines until Jim or Dad could assist me in my choice. It wasn't long before Dad came walking out of the stables with the trail guide leading a buckskin mare towards me. My goodness, the horse seemed enormous! As they approached, the guide said, "Donna, meet Sunshine."

"Sunshine. Is that the horse's name?"

"Well, it ain't my name." He gave me a lopsided grin.

"I know that," I said. "Isn't he awfully big?"

"First of all, he's a she. Secondly, this mare is the gentlest, calmest, best-natured horse in the whole stables. I understand you haven't ridden before. Sunshine is the perfect horse for people who want to go slow and easy."

"Well, I guess that would be me."

I looked over at my Dad for some kind of indication of support. He nodded his head to assure me the choice was good.

"Well, young lady, let's get you up on this horse," said the guide.

"How do I do that? I'm too short to throw my leg up that high."

"You are built a bit close to the ground. We'll have to use a mounting block."

"What's that?"

"You and your Dad wait right here, and I'll be back in a couple of shakes."

I turned to my father, "Dad do something. I'm not sure this is such a good idea."

"Don't worry, Donna, the trail guide knows what he's doing. Relax, once you are up on Sunshine that whole world will seem different."

Oh, yeah, once I'm 'up on Sunshine' I'll be stranded on the biggest horse in the world, I thought to myself.

The trail guide returned within minutes, and he was carrying this wooden box that had steps attached to it. He put it down beside Sunshine. The horse didn't bat an eyelash, or even move. I guess she was used to people mounting her from a box.

"Just climb up there, and I'll help you get up into the saddle," the guide instructed.

It wasn't as hard as I expected. He boosted me up and on the saddle by lifting me with his hands under my left foot. It happened very fast. I was sitting on a horse!

"Now, grip the barrel of the horse with your legs," he said.

"Where's the barrel?" I asked.

"The barrel is the round stomach area."

I tried, but my legs stuck straight out with no ability to bend or grip anything. They were just too short.

"Now what do I do?"

"Hm-m-m, this is a small problem. Oh well, do the best you can and go *real* slow. Keep Sunshine to an even walk, and try not to let her trot or gallop, okay?"

I nodded my head in assent. He continued, "when you want to go right, gently pull on the rein on her right side, and when you want to go left, pull on the other side. When you want to stop her, pull directly back on both reins. When you want her to go forward, loosen the reins in your hands and say 'git-up.' If she won't go, gently nudge her forward with the heels of your shoes. Got it?"

I nodded my head.

"Okay, you try to take her through the different movements."

Sunshine was very easy to manage. In fact, she anticipated my instructions in advance and lazily went right then left, she stopped agreeably, and went forward without any "nudging" from me. I was quickly getting to like that horse. I sat as straight as I could in the saddle, and joined in the line of the other riders headed to the trail along the Old Beach Road.

*   *   *

As dark descended, the night skies turned spectacular. There were no clouds obscuring the full moon or the spattering of thousands of twinkling stars. It was amazing.

Sunshine plodded along with little resistance, following the horse in front of her. Every now and then she would kind of snort and shake her head rapidly from side to side. Then she would completely stop. I would give her a little prod, say "git up," and give her the reins. Each time we went through this routine, she would immediately start walking again. Because of these pauses, we were getting behind the rest of the group. I gave her a little slap on her backside to hurry her along. She broke into a trot. Oh my goodness, that was not the thing to do. It had not been comfortable riding Sunshine from step one. When she went down, I seemed to go up, and we would meet somewhere in the middle. When she broke into a trot, it was three times as bad and three times more often. It must have been annoying to her as well, because she settled back into a walk very quickly, making those snorting sounds for several minutes. I decided lagging behind was preferable to being bounced to death. When everyone stopped to have our hot dog roast, Sunshine and I caught up.

Dad helped me get off my horse. To my surprise, when my feet hit solid ground, I could barely stand up. My legs were shaking. Dad softly laughed at me, and told me that it was very common to be weak-legged after riding a horse, and I would be fine in a few minutes. He was right about that, but I was also worried about how I was going to get back up onto Sunshine when it came time to return to the stables.

*   *   *

The hot dog roast was a lot of fun. After eating, we sat around the campfire and sang songs like *Kumbayah* and *Michael Row Your Boat Ashore* (it was the 1960's). Then the girls cleaned up the picnic area, and the boys made sure the fire was totally out. It was time to get back up on Sunshine.

The guide led my horse over to me, and, to my surprise, he had a small, sturdy fold out ladder gadget with him that I could use like a mounting block. When he set the ladder next to Sunshine, she suddenly pulled back, snorting and stomping her front feet. It took three people to get me up on that horse: one to hold her head, one to hold the silly little ladder, and one to boost me up and onto her back. Frankly, it was embarrassing. The guide stuttered around apologizing for Sunshine's behavior. According to him, she had never acted that badly before. Now that I was mounted, I just wanted to get going back to the stables.

Sunshine was not a happy horse. She barely moved, and continued snorting her protests. I was getting further and further behind the group. Finally she completely stopped and refused to go one more step forward. Jim pulled out of line and came back beside us to grab her reins and lead her on. No way was she going to tolerate being bullied. She whipped her head around and bit him on the foot!

Jim let out a loud yell that brought the trail guide galloping back to where we were at a standstill. He was completely flustered over the "accident," and his primary concern was to get Jim back to the stables and get his foot tended. Sunshine had not broken the skin on Jim's foot, but it was badly bruised and throbbing. We all knew the bite would swell, and Jim needed to get his shoe off and his foot elevated as quickly as possible.

Dad had joined us too. The guide decided to have him take Jim immediately back to the stables and then over to the base clinic to have his foot checked. About the time they left, Sunshine decided she would walk forward again. The guide had to return to the front of the line, because his horse was the lead animal. He ascertained that I would be fine, following them at the end of the line of riders. Sunshine did know her way back, and he instructed me to let her go at her own speed.

Off we went again, step by slow step. The rest of the group was getting further ahead of me by every passing minute. Oh well, what could I do but just hope that Sunshine knew where she was going. She was still snorting and shaking her head, but she had not stopped walking ... yet.

I could barely see the last rider in line, and had not glimpsed the light from the stables, when Sunshine decided enough is enough. She stopped! I tried and tried to prod her forward, but every time I nudged her with my heels, she snorted loudly. I was stuck, alone with a horse in the Libyan Desert. I didn't know what to do.

The warnings the guide had given us (before we left) about adders and cobras in the sand were shouting in my mind. He said our horse would shy away from a snake and get out of striking range before he/she would go around it. In other words, let the horse take its rider to safety, and not vice versa.

That's all fine and good, but what if your horse wouldn't move? I was starting to panic. Why was Sunshine acting like that? I knew the answer to my question: if I were Sunshine, I wouldn't put up with some dumb human bouncing up and down of my back for hours. It must have hurt her, and she was getting as sore as I was. If I wanted that horse to move, I had to get off of her! I also knew that, once on the ground, there was no way I was getting back onto Sunshine on my own. I gritted my teeth and jumped to my feet. My legs went temporarily useless, but recovered quickly. I took the reins and started to lead her forward. To my relief, Sunshine agreeably started to walk. In fact, she got a little ahead of me, and was leading me back to the stables.

The stables weren't as far away as I thought they were, and the guide had turned back to find me after he got the other riders safely situated. I did not get back up on Sunshine, but walked her back the rest of the way. I didn't have a lot to say to the trail guide, and neither did Sunshine.

Jim's foot was black and blue for weeks, and he limped around a lot, but it healed perfectly. I told him I was "sorry" so often, he got tired of hearing it.

I didn't get any blisters or saddle sores, but I still learned a good lesson. Some of us adventurers were never designed to ride a horse, and for the betterment of both the animal and us, it's best to either walk or ride a bike to where we want to go. I never saw Sunshine again. I didn't really miss her, and, I'm sure, she never missed me.

"A lady will never accost a strange man in public."

—Bernice DeMuth

Anchors Aweigh

... as told by Pat

Homeroom had to be the most boring period of the school day. Thankfully, it was only fifteen minutes long—time enough to take attendance, recite the Pledge of Allegiance, and cover the announcements for the day. I sat twiddling my pencil as the principal's voice droned out at us from the P.A. speakers.

"... this week's meeting of the Chess Club has been changed to Thursday. Now, a note that should be of interest to all of you."

This was something different—I perked up a bit to actually listen.

"Next week, the U.S.S. Franklin D. Roosevelt and its escort will be docking at Tripoli harbor. They will be assigned here for a period of two weeks. We are making arrangements for field trips to the aircraft carrier, and setting up a schedule ..."

Outside, a distant rumble quickly grew to a thunderous roar that crested right above the school and interrupted him, making all the windows rattle. No one in the room even glanced up; such interruptions were frequent and common when you attended school on a SAC airbase. The end of the flight line was located about a half mile behind the school, and they were scrambling jets into the air again. We were convinced that the pilots used the school roof as a visual signal to hit their after-burners.

The principal picked up in mid-sentence as the thunder faded, right where he had been before the interruption. "Yes, let's see, a schedule for all of you to have the chance to visit the ship. Also, the crews will be given shore liberty, and we expect to see several of the seamen here on base. The USO is preparing activities for that time, and I want to remind all of you to be polite and respectful to these guests of Wheelus." He spoke very rapidly as he delivered the last half of the announcement, wanting to get in his say before the next roar, now rumbling in the distance, could blot him out again. When they were scrambling jets, they launched four to six groups of three jets each, about a minute apart.

As the second roar faded into the distance, the bell rang, releasing us for the five-minute break between classes. As we gathered up our books and headed for our first class, everyone was talking about the imminent arrival of the aircraft carrier. The boys were eagerly discussing technology and artillery while the girls were more interested in the hundreds of sailors expected to soon be wandering around Wheelus.

Over the next few days, excitement rose as plans were made for the arrival of the Navy. The base theater published a schedule of an assortment of movies to be played in rotation. The USO scheduled four buffets and heavily chaperoned dances for each of the two weeks that the ships would be berthed in Tripoli, and issued an open invitation to all the high school girls to act as hostesses. The Officer's club, NCO club, and Airmen's club announced that they would be open to all rank-appropriate Navy personnel. This announcement delighted my older brother—Jim picked up a lot of pocket money by shooting pool at the Airmen's club, and the prospect of numerous new victims who didn't know him was like hitting the lottery.

Finally, the day arrived. As the school bus trundled along the road next to Tripoli harbor, we could all clearly see the two destroyers anchored there. The aircraft carrier, much too large to fit inside the harbor walls, was anchored a short distance out to sea, but still easily visible. The three ships were proudly flying the American flag, and the bus erupted with cheers that were quickly followed by a loud and spirited rendition of *What Do You Do With a Drunken Sailor?* The Navy had docked.

*   *   *

"So, how was the dance last night?" I asked my sister, Donna. Since she was in high school, she qualified as a USO hostess.

"It was fun. They had one of the guys from the base radio station as a deejay, and I danced almost every dance. And look at this: I got two sailor hats." She pulled out her drawer on the desk, and showed me the hats.

"Oh. Well, yeah, that does sound like fun. Did Bobbie and Sharon have fun, too?"

"Yep. Bobbie collected four hats, and she's got a date to go to the movies this weekend with this really cute guy she met."

Donna and I were in our bedroom. She was sitting at the desk painting her nails, and I was lying on my bed. I twisted around and sat up, Indian-style, so I could see her while we talked. I hesitated a moment, and then asked, "Are you guys going to go to any more of the dances?"

"Yeah, we're going to the one tomorrow night."

"Is Dad going to take you?"

"No, Mr. Welch is going to take us out to the base and bring us back. Dad took us last night."

I hesitated again, and then ventured, "Could I come with you guys?"

"What?"

"Can I come, too? I could tell Mom and Dad I was going to the library or something, and if you let me use some of your makeup ..."

"No way. You're not old enough to be at the USO."

"Well, I'm almost old enough! And I don't think it's fair that it's only the high school girls who get to go. We have dances at the junior high. They should let us go, too."

"Well, they're not going to, and Dad would kill me if he found out that I even thought about sneaking you in."

"But, everyone says I look older than I am, and with some makeup and maybe a pair of your heels ..."

"I doubt that you could even *walk* in heels, much less dance. Besides, those sailors are way too old for you."

"They're not that old. I've seen them around base, and most of them look like they're about Jim's age."

"And Jim is five years older than you. Those sailors have to be at least eighteen to even join up, so that makes them at least six years older than you. No, sorry, you're still too young for this, and I am not going to risk getting grounded for the rest of my life by sneaking you into one of those dances. Just drop it, okay?"

"Okay," I muttered. I waited a minute or so before I asked, "So, why did you get those hats?"

"All the girls are trying to collect sailor hats; it's cool. They're kinda like heart-break trophies."

"How do you get them to give you their hats? Isn't that part of their uniform?"

"Sure it is. But you just act friendly and interested in them, compliment them, flirt a little bit, and then suggest that you'd like something to remember them by—like their hat." Donna turned to me with a big grin. "Tomorrow night I'm going to try to get a neckerchief."

"And all the girls are doing this? Collecting hats?"

"If they want to be cool they are."

"Well, I still think if you let me come tomorrow night …"

"No, no, and no again. Even if the chaperones didn't catch you, the other girls all know that you're my kid sister and not old enough. This whole idea is not cool!" She waved her fingers in the air to help dry the polish, and then got up and left the room.

I flopped back down on my bed and stared at the ceiling, thinking hard. I desperately wanted to be included in all the fun, and to prove that I was as "cool" as any of the high school kids. I would just have to think of an alternate way to do that.

Like all adolescents, I believed that I was extremely mature and in control of myself. It was apparent to me that the USO chaperones were dreadfully old-fashioned, and didn't have the flexibility to make allowances for prodigies such as myself. There was no way that I would admit that I was being motivated by jealousy, or that the idea of crashing the USO dance was pretty stupid. Instead, I was feeling wrongfully misunderstood and categorized, but I couldn't see a way to break down the resistance ranked against me.

I mulled over the problem some more, but no stunningly brilliant solutions were coming to me. Well, I would just have to work on it.

*   *   *

By the next day, I had formulated a plan. Without realizing it, Donna had given me an idea. Even if I couldn't go to the dances, I was determined to collect some sailor hats to prove how cool I was.

When school let out for the day, I waited by the school buses for either Donna or Jim to show up. In a few minutes, I spotted Jim coming down the street from the high school. As usual, a group of friends surrounded him. I took a deep breath and walked over to interrupt the group.

"Hey, Jim, are you taking the bus home?"

"What? Oh, hey there, Twerp." I flinched. *How* could he call me that stupid nickname in front of a bunch of high school kids?

"Yeah, anyway, are you going home now?" I asked him.

"Yeah, I thought I would. Why?"

"I need you to tell Mom that I'm staying on base. I'm going over to the library, and I'll come home with Dad when he gets off. Okay?"

"Oh, sure, no problem." He turned back to his group of friends.

Stage One completed.

I quickly walked the few blocks to Dad's office where I dropped off my schoolbooks and told him that I was going to the library. He reminded me that he got off at five o'clock and would not appreciate waiting around for me. I agreed to keep an eye on the time and left his office with a cheery wave.

Stage Two completed.

The airbase was full of sailors wandering around, and I was loose in the middle of it—unsupervised and unchaperoned—for an hour and a half. I strolled down the street, observing carefully as I prepared to select my first victim. I decided against approaching a group of sailors—I felt I would do better if I found one who was alone. And I didn't want a really good-looking one, strolling along oozing confidence. I kept walking.

Stage Three implemented and in progress.

Then I spotted him! There was a young sailor walking towards me. He looked like he was barely eighteen, had a military haircut, wore glasses, and carried his sailor's hat seated squarely on his head rather than worn at a cocky angle. I quickly reviewed what Donna had said the night before. First, act friendly and interested in them.

The sailor was now about six feet from me. I pasted a bright smile on my face and said, "Hi! Welcome to Wheelus. Can I help you find something, like the library or the BX?"

The sailor looked startled to be accosted in this way, but he recovered quickly and stopped walking. "Oh, um-m, hi, kid. I'm not really looking for anything. Just thought I'd see what the base was like. Thanks, anyway."

Before he could start off again, I moved to the second step—compliment them about something. I quickly scanned him and then added, "Wow, your shoes are sure shiny! I don't think I've ever seen shoes look that good."

He glanced down at his feet in confusion, then looked back at me like I had lost my mind. "Well, uh-h-h, thanks, I guess."

Step three—flirt with them a little. I leaned in a little bit, gave him another toothpaste smile, and fluttered my eyelashes at him.

"Hey, kid, are you okay? Do you have something in your eye?"

I now bestowed a wide-eyed gaze on him and moved in for the kill. "Oh, no, I'm fine. Can I have your hat to remember you by?"

"No, you can't have my hat!" He stepped back quickly, lifting his left hand to clutch his hat to his head. "Look, kid, uh-h-h, it was real nice meeting you, but I gotta go. I'm, um-m-m, I'm meeting some friends." He spun on his heel and took off back the way he had come, walking very rapidly.

I watched his quickly retreating back as I reviewed the encounter in my mind. I couldn't understand why he hadn't cooperated. I had done everything that Donna had said to do. I decided that perhaps I had picked a sailor who was little *too* dorky to understand the finer points of flirting. I continued on my way, seeking another victim upon whom to practice my charms.

By the time I returned to Dad's office at five, I had managed to run off seven sailors, and I was still hatless. On the ride home, I sat in the front seat in a silent funk. When Dad asked me why I didn't have any library books, I just told him that I couldn't find anything interesting. Since the base library was large and very well stocked, and since I usually returned with the maximum allowed of four books out at a time, this comment earned a surprised and confused look from Dad. He asked me if I felt okay, and I mumbled something incomprehensible in reply. That little exchange explained why Mom insisted on taking my temperature later that night.

Disappointed but still determined, I decided to continue my quest for a sailor's hat. I stayed on base after school for the next two afternoons, walking around until my legs ached while I pestered sailor after sailor.

On the third afternoon, which was a Friday, I approached my second sailor for the day. I had no more than started my "Hi. Welcome to Wheelus." routine when he started laughing and said, "Hey! Are you that kid who's running around trying to get hats?"

"What?" I replied, startled.

"There's some crazy blonde kid here on base who keeps trying to get guys to give her their hats. I thought it might be you."

"I don't know anything about that," I said loftily. "I'm on my way to the base library to get some books, but I thought I'd welcome you to Tripoli."

"Oh, well, okay. Thanks. See ya, kid." With that, the sailor strolled off.

The encounter shook me a little. Apparently, sailors told tales and were not gentlemen about their dealings with ladies. My cover as a seductive vamp was blown, and I figured there was now zero chance of getting a hat. Also, one of those idiots might have gone so far as to inform the MP's of my activities, and I could picture myself arrested and locked up in the brig. When Dad learned the details, he would be so disgusted with me that he probably wouldn't even try to get me out. With a sigh, I headed for the library. When I returned to Dad's office at five, I was lugging my normal load of four books.

*   *   *

On Sunday evening, Donna and I were again in our bedroom talking. The FDR and its escort had now been in Tripoli for a week, half of the time they were assigned to be there. Sailor hats were showing up over at the high school—worn by girls, hung casually but prominently on hooks in girls' lockers, or negligently carried about on top of a stack of schoolbooks in a girl's arms. Donna's collection now featured five hats and two neckerchiefs. She had attended three of the USO dances, had gone on two movie dates, and, on the previous Thursday, had been with her class on their field trip to the aircraft carrier. We were talking about the field trip.

"What was it like, being out there on that boat?" I asked.

"First of all, you don't call it a boat. It's a ship. They used some *boats* called launches to pick us up at the harbor and take us out to the ship."

"All right, so what was the *ship* like?"

"Huge. It's like a floating city or something. It's so big that you don't even feel any motion from the waves. Even though it's anchored outside the harbor, it was as steady as a rock."

"Really?"

"Yeah. Well, it's big enough to have a runway on the top deck, isn't it? And I think they said the crew was something like about three thousand sailors."

"Wow! Did you get to see all of it?"

"Most of it. We were out there half the day. They showed us the engines and all that stuff, and where they store the planes and stuff. The planes are neat—the wings fold up to make them more compact for when they're not using them. They even launched one of the planes for us. There's this big sling-shot thing that practically shoots the planes off the runway, and when they land there's this other hook thing that catches the bottom of the plane and stops it before it crashes at the end of the runway."

"Is that all they show you? The engines and planes?"

"No, they also gave us a tour of the crew quarters, the mess-hall, and stuff like that. It's so big that they even have a theater, a great big gym, a sick bay that's as big as a small hospital, and a store kinda like the BX where the sailors can shop. It really is like a small city."

"Why would the sailors need a store? What kind of stuff do they sell?"

"Like I said, it's a lot like the BX. They had books and magazines, and a whole section for records, record players, and radios. There was another section full of snack stuff, and a big section where they sell uniforms and stuff."

"I thought the Navy gave them their uniforms?"

"They do, but this was stuff like tailored uniforms, belt buckles with a picture of the ship on them, extra neckerchiefs and hats and stuff. You know, it's like Dad did. The Air Force gave him his basic uniforms, but you know he bought some more,"

"Oh, yeah, he did, didn't he? What else did they have?"

"Oh, souvenir stuff, and postcards—all kinds of things."

"Can we buy stuff in there?"

"Yeah, some of the kids were buying souvenirs. I didn't see anything I wanted, though. I thought the souvenirs were kind of expensive for what you get."

"Our field trip isn't until next Wednesday. It sounds like fun, though."

"It was. And it was really interesting. You'll like it. Well, I have to do some homework now. I have to read three chapters in this book." Donna turned back to the desk and opened a book. I picked up my library book and went out to the living room so I wouldn't disturb her.

I sat with my book open in my lap, but I wasn't reading. In my mind, I was turning over the conversation with my sister and cooking up another plan to acquire a hat. I had some money saved up, and I hoped it would be enough. When I went on my field trip I would buy a hat from the ship's store. Then, I could stencil some guy's name inside of it (something like "Smith, John") and pretend that I had acquired it through my charms. It would be a real sailor's hat, no one would know the difference, and I would be proven to be as "cool" as anyone else. Suddenly, I was really looking forward to my field trip.

*　　*　　*

Wednesday dawned gray and stormy—unusual weather for Tripoli. Overnight an autumn storm had blown in across the Mediterranean bringing heavily overcast skies, rainsqualls, and wind. As the school bus drove along the coast road, we could see that the usually placid, blue sea was iron gray and choppy, with whitecaps showing far out from shore. By the time we arrived at school, those of us in the seventh grade were beginning to worry that our field trip might be canceled.

Our Homeroom teacher was quick to reassure us that we would indeed have our field trip. The bus for the harbor would be leaving right after an early lunch. However, since the seas were so rough, we wouldn't be going out to the aircraft carrier. We would instead tour one of the two destroyers that were anchored in the comparatively calm harbor. As we all started to groan in disappointment, the teacher rapped the desk for silence and told us that the principal was trying to arrange an additional second trip for us if time and weather permitted before the aircraft carrier left. Well, touring one of the destroyers was still better than spending the afternoon in classes.

We arrived at the harbor to find three Navy launches waiting to take us to our ship. The sailors quickly and efficiently divided us among the boats, and then started for the destroyer. The small American flags on each boat were snapping in the wind, and the prows of the launches were slapping up and down against the waves. Even though the harbor was more protected than the sea, it was still much rougher than normal.

When we arrived, we had to transfer from the launch to a steep, narrow steel stairway that went up the side of the destroyer. That was pretty scary, but the sailors were helpful and held on to each of us until they were sure we were firmly on the stairs. On the deck, another group of four sailors who were going to be our guides met us. They welcomed us to the ship and told us its name and a little of the ship's history. I have to admit that I don't even remember the ship's name.

The tour started deep in the ship in the engine room, a hot, noisy place that reeked of engine oil and diesel fumes. From there, we were led through the ship, gradually ascending deck by deck as we were shown the crew quarters, the mess hall, the sick bay, and other "attractions." The air seemed stuffy and hot to me, and there was a pervading odor of metal and oil everywhere. The corridors were narrow, and for some reason it seemed hard to walk through them without bumping into the walls. I was getting a bad headache and finding it hard to pay attention.

We finally arrived back on the top deck, and I gratefully gulped in some deep breaths of fresh air. Our guides pointed out the artillery cannons. That got the boys in our group very excited and asking stupid questions like how many people each shell could kill. I was bored to death, and in all that touring I had not spotted anything like a ship's store. I did notice that one of our guides seemed to be watching me a lot, but my headache was getting worse and I didn't feel up to flirting. I came up with a wan smile for him, but that was the best I could do.

As we moved along the deck the next item of interest to be pointed out was the mast. Even though ships no longer carried canvas sails, they still had masts, which now supported a large array of communication equipment and antennas. As I gazed up at it, I realized that I could also see the mast on the other destroyer anchored right next door. In fact, I could see the two masts moving in a slow dance. They slowly swayed towards each other, then apart, and then back again. Suddenly, my head was splitting and my stomach gave a little lurch. I closed my eyes for a second, but it didn't help.

The sailor who had been watching me grabbed my arm and began dragging me away from the group. I tried to resist, but found that I didn't have the strength. We were headed for the side of the ship. As we hit the railing, he yelled, "Over the side, kid!"

I grabbed the railing and reared back. "Wait! Don't I get a plank for this?" I yelled back.

"Not for this!" He pushed my head and shoulders over the railing and repeated, "Over the side!"

I found myself looking down the steep gray side of the destroyer and noticed waves lapping and foaming against the hull at the waterline. My stomach lurched again, and everything I had eaten that day made a rapid exit from my system. Clamped to the railing like a barnacle, I gagged and retched and spit, trying to clear my mouth. I felt too horrible to even be actively embarrassed. Beside me, I heard the sailor's voice say, "Try not to get it on the deck."

After a few minutes, the retching stopped. I was dripping in sweat and my legs felt like they were made of marshmallow. Still clutching the railing, I slowly straightened up. The sailor was still next to me, but when I looked at him he kept dividing into two and then merging back to about one and a half.

"Are you okay now?" the sailor asked me.

"I … I think so …" I looked around, trying to orient myself, and the first thing I saw were those two masts slowly swaying towards each other again. With a groan, I hung my head back over the side. This time, everything I had eaten for the past week seemed to be making an exit. I briefly wondered if it was possible to puke up your toenails, because it certainly felt like that was what I was trying to do.

When I finally straightened up, shaking and trembling had been added to my other symptoms. The sailor beside me had conjured up a paper cup of water from somewhere and handed it to me silently. I rinsed my mouth and then, in a very unladylike way, spit over the side. I took a small sip of the water, and looked back at the sailor. This time, at least, he stayed in focus.

"Thanks," I said. Then I heard myself say, "Can I have your hat?"

"My hat? Why do you want my hat?"

I was too sick and dispirited to do anything but tell the truth. "Because it's cool. All the high school girls are getting them, and my sister has five, and I've been trying, and ... Oh, never mind. I think I need to sit down"

"I think you do, too." He led me back along the deck and seated me on some kind of locker or box thing that was very close to the stairs we had climbed when coming aboard. He said, "Okay, you just stay there. The tour's almost over, and your class will come back here to disembark. The railing is right there if you start feeling, well, you know." He pointed out the railing for me, and then left to rejoin the field trip.

I sat there and waited, trying to ignore the slight sway of the deck beneath me. I didn't care any more about hats, sailors, ships, or being cool. All I wanted was to feel solid ground beneath my feet again, and then to find somewhere cool and dim to lie down. The nurse's office at school was suddenly a very appealing place. I sat there in a stupor, waiting for my class to return.

After about fifteen minutes, I could hear the chatter of my classmates as they returned to the stairs. The stupid boys were *still* carrying on about the cannons, sinking ships, and killing people. I pushed myself to my feet and looked over at the group. I spotted several smirks among them, and knew that the story of my seasickness was already spreading. My face flamed scarlet.

I shuffled into line to wait for my turn on the stairs. My legs were still a little shaky, and I was praying that I could get down the steps without falling into the harbor and drowning myself. As we inched along, I found that my stomach did better if I kept my eyes on the solid land across the harbor.

There were only four people in front of me when I heard a voice call, "Hey, kid!" I ignored it. Now there were only three people until it was my turn to leave. The voice called again, "Hey, kid! Wait a minute!" I glanced around and saw the sailor who had helped me striding towards me. I wanted to push the three kids in front of me overboard so I could get off the ship before he drew any more attention to me. The next thing I knew, he was beside me saying, "Here. You forgot something." He pushed some kind of fabric into my hand. I figured it was probably a napkin in case I puked again before I got across the harbor. I had never been so humiliated before in my life.

I muttered, "thanks," without looking at either him or whatever it was he had given me. He patted my shoulder and walked away.

I didn't look at what I had in my hand until we were back in the bus going back to school. There, clutched in my fist, was a scrunched up sailor's hat. I straightened it out carefully and found, stenciled on the inside, the name "Miller, Chas." I put the hat on and grinned as I realized that *some* sailors were gentlemen, after all.

"Denial is a river in Egypt."

—Raymond DeMuth

First Kiss

… as told by Donna

I burst into the house, slamming the heavy wooden door of our villa behind me, and headed down the hall at a full run. My destination was the sink in the bathroom.

I turned on the water and grabbed my toothbrush. I frantically rummaged around in the cupboard beneath the sink until I found what I was looking for. I had not heard my mother hurry down the hall after me. Just as I was applying the "tooth cleaner" onto my toothbrush, she cried out, "Donna, stop! What are you doing!? You aren't going to brush your teeth with that, are you!?

"Why not?" I asked.

She grabbed the can of Ajax™ scouring cleanser out of my hand. "This is poison! Look at what it says on the outside of the can! *If accidentally swallowed, seek medical help immediately.*"

"Oh," I said in small voice.

"What is the matter with you—what were you thinking?"

"I wanted to get my teeth totally cleaned."

"And regular toothpaste wouldn't work?" Mom asked, still bewildered by my actions.

"No, I need to use something special. Something that will get them super clean."

"Use the toothpaste, and then rinse with Listerine™."

"How much Listerine™ can I use?"

"You can use the whole bottle, if you want. If you swallow too much, you'll just get a tummy ache."

"All right. Thanks. Can I be alone now to brush my teeth?"

Mom left the room and shut the door behind her. I thought she had left and gone back into the living room, but she was waiting outside the bathroom door when I came out.

Standing there with her arms folded across her chest, she said, "Would you like to explain yourself now, and tell me what happened that made you want to brush your teeth with Ajax™, for God's sake."

I looked straight at her. "No! I can't talk about it. It's too horrible to say!" I cried, and covered my face with my hands. I hurried past her and darted back down the hall to my room.

*   *   *

I was curled up on my side on my bed, my face to the wall. I was confused and worried, but most of all I was in turmoil. *What had happened? And why me? What did he think he was doing? How can I talk to someone about this? I can't tell Mom, she might think it was my fault. What if she told Dad? Can I trust her to understand?*

I lay there on my bed with all these thoughts going through my head. The time quickly ticked by. My little sister came in to go to bed, and I pretended I was asleep. Jim came home and went into his room. I heard Dad tell Mom he was "retiring for the night," and he went to their room. The house was very quiet. I could finally get up, and at least get myself something to drink.

As I walked into the kitchen, I heard a small movement in the living room. I went to investigate the sound. There was my Mother, sitting by herself in the quiet, waiting (I knew) for me.

"Come in, Sweetheart, and sit down and talk with me," she said.

I went in the room and sat in the chair next to her, but I didn't say a word.

"Whenever you're ready to talk, I'm ready to listen."

I looked into her eyes—I knew she wanted to help me. No harm would come my way if I trusted her.

"Promise me you won't get mad, or, worse yet, laugh at me."

"I promise, Donna."

I took a deep breath, and then began to talk. "As you know, Bobbie, Sharon (my two best friends) and I went to a movie tonight, and after the movie we decided to go over to the base annex." (The annex was kind of like a hamburger/soda shop, where the teenagers and young airmen could go. It had a small dance floor and a jukebox. No alcohol was served there.) "It's a neat place to meet new boys. Dance a little and listen to music."

"We were having a good time, and I met this young guy whose name was Gary. He was fun to talk to, and seemed to like me too. After dancing a couple times, he asked me if I wanted to get some fresh air. I said 'yeah' and went outside with him. I knew he wanted to be alone with me, and he seemed okay. He said I was pretty, and had neat hair. He asked me if he could kiss me. I said that would be all right. He put his arms around me, and started to give me a kiss."

"Oh, Mom, I can't believe what he did!"

"It's okay, Donna, just tell me what happened next."

"He put his tongue in my mouth! Oh, gross! Oh, yuck! I think he's a pervert! Why would he want to do that!"

The words continued to spew out. "Can I get some horrible kind of disease from him? That's why I was going to use Ajax™. I thought it would kill the germs! Mom, tell me the truth! Am I going to die!

"No, dear, you are not going to die. Calm down. Everything will be just fine."

She put her hand out and took mine. She gently patted my hand, looked straight into my eyes, and said, "I should have explained this to you before now. You are growing up so fast; I guess time just got past me. I'm sorry, honey. What you experienced tonight is quite natural."

"What! You mean to tell me boys are supposed to do that!"

"Well, I wouldn't say they are supposed to kiss like that, but a lot of them do. Normally, it would be older boys. But things are changing, and teenagers are experimenting earlier—a lot earlier—than we did when I was your age. That doesn't mean that you have to kiss that way, if you're not ready. In fact, it's wiser to wait until you are older."

"What is that kind of kiss called?"

"It's called a French kiss."

"So, that's what a French kiss is. What is wrong with the French? It's gross! I'm glad I'm not French. Do they drool every time they kiss someone?"

Mom softly laughed at my reaction. "No, they kiss regularly, too."

"Well, I'll tell you this. I'm not fond of French kisses, and I think I'll just stick to good old American kisses.

"What did you say to that young man, Donna?"

"Well, I pushed him away, and told him that, if he wanted to get his face all wet, he could go soak his head! Then I left."

We sat silently for a minute or two.

"Mom, please don't tell Dad. I don't think he will understand."

"No, I won't tell him. This will be between you and me, if you promise not to make me wait and worry so long until you tell me what's bothering you. Deal?

"Okay, deal. Well … I think I'll go to bed now."

"You sure you're all right, and you'll be able to go to sleep?"

"Yeah, and thanks for staying up and talking to me. I love you, Mom."

"I love you, too, Sweetheart. Goodnight."

*   *   *

The trauma didn't last too long after that. I did, though, have some bad dreams that night. I dreamt about snakes, lizards, anteaters, and, oh yeah, about frogs too … a really dumb dream about frogs.

"Why would you want to be like everybody else? It would be an extremely boring world if everyone were the same."

—Bernice DeMuth

A Two-Camel Woman

... as told by Pat

We had a lot of different experiences while we were in Libya, but one event has always stood out from the others. That event was so unique that the telling of it quickly grew to the status of a family legend. I am referring, of course, to the time that Dad sold Donna to an Arab.

It all began very innocently. One afternoon, Mom decided to take my little brother and go for a walk in the neighborhood. She got Ray situated in his stroller, took him outside, and carefully locked the door behind her. She then told our houseboy, Massoud, that she would be back soon.

Halfway through her walk, she was approached by a young Arab man. He appeared to be in his late teens or early twenties, and he was neatly and carefully dressed in Western-style clothing. He was very nervous about speaking to an unaccompanied woman in the street, but he was extremely polite and respectful. He introduced himself, saying that his name was Bubaka, and explained that he was a student who had just completed his upper level classes (somewhat equivalent to our high schools). Though he spoke English, he wasn't fluent in it, and he was aware of his shortcomings. He was looking for an American family who might be interested in helping him to perfect his language skills.

Mom considered the young man and his proposal for a few moments while she quickly reviewed what she knew of Arab culture. She replied that the idea seemed a good one to her, but she could not make such a decision. Bubaka would need to come to our house and speak with her husband about it. Naturally, her husband was the only person with the authority to make such a decision for the family. Bubaka understood completely, and seemed reassured that the woman he had chosen to speak to was such a respectful and proper wife.

94

Mom let him accompany her home so that he would know where our house was. At the door, she arranged with him to return on Thursday evening at seven o'clock so that he could speak with Dad.

Over dinner that evening, Mom told all of us about her encounter. We discussed it for a few minutes, and decided it might be interesting to see what the young man had in mind. However, first we had to see if he would return on Thursday evening.

*   *   *

On Thursday evening, we all waited in anticipation for our visitor. Mom had arranged the living room in a way that she hoped would be appropriate. Dad's chair was in its usual place with the couch to his right. The second armchair, intended for Mom, had been placed to Dad's left and slightly behind his chair, and two dining room chairs had been added to the side and rear of Mom's chair. A pot of coffee was perking in the kitchen, and a large plate of freshly baked cookies was waiting on a tray with Mom's best dessert service.

At the stroke of seven there was a tentative knock on our front door. Jim jumped to his feet and answered the door. There was Bubaka, looking both nervous and excited as he stood outside the door. When he saw Jim, he bowed his head slightly and said, "Good evening to thee, good sir. I am Bubaka. Did your lady-wife tell you about me?"

Jim smiled in reply and said, "My mother told us about you. My name is Jim."

"Ah, I meant no disrespect or offense. Thy mother seemed too young to have a son of such age."

"No offense taken. Please, won't you come in and meet my father? You're expected, and our family is waiting for you." Jim stepped back and opened the door wide in invitation. Bubaka stepped inside and looked around with wide eyes, and then followed Jim into the living room.

Dad stood up and shook hands with Bubaka as Jim introduced them. The three of them then sat down, Dad in his chair and Bubaka and Jim seated on the couch to his right. Mom came in quietly with the tray of coffee and cookies, which she placed on the coffee table, then seated herself in the chair slightly behind Dad. Dad formally introduced her, and then he called Donna and me into the room. We brought our little brother, Raymond, with us. We were introduced in turn and Donna and I seated ourselves in the two chairs behind Mom. Raymond, not quite four years old, clambered up into Mom's lap.

The first few minutes were very awkward—no one seemed to know what to say to "break the ice." Bubaka seemed to be very nervous about being in a room with three unveiled women, and he would not look directly at Mom, Donna, or me. Instead, he focused his attention on Dad, which promptly made Dad very nervous. Dad smiled at Bubaka, cleared his throat once or twice, and said, "Well, here we all are …"

Jim came to everyone's rescue by beginning, "Bubaka, we want to welcome you to our home. Mother has told us a little about you, and that you would like help with your English. Can you tell us a little more of what you have in mind?"

"Ah, yes, I thank thee. As I told thy lady-mother, I have worked very hard to complete school and learn much that I can use to better myself. I would like to gain employment with the oil companies, or perhaps on the American air-base. To this end, I learned English, but I find now that I do not sound like others when I speak. I have sought other classes, but have not found such. I thought if I could talk with Americans, I could discover my error and …" He looked around at us hopefully.

"That makes a great deal of sense," said Mom, directing her comments to Dad. "The best way to learn a language is to speak it."

"Right," said Dad. "But what do we talk about? And when would we do it? What did you have in mind, Bubaka?"

Bubaka spread his hands and looked at Dad in confusion. Perhaps he had been afraid that his hopes would be shot down before he ever got to this point, and he hadn't formulated his ideas beyond gaining an audience for his request. He shook his head, and appeared to be searching for words.

Once again, Jim stepped in. "Well, we're very interested in Libya, and the culture and traditions here. It's very different from our home. Perhaps Bubaka could tell us about his country?" Bubaka nodded eagerly, and Jim continued, "And we could tell him about our country and culture. We could all learn a great deal about each other, which is the first step to becoming friends."

"Yes, yes!" cried Bubaka. "The son of thine house, Jeem, he has put my wish into words. If I could come here and spend time speaking with all of thee, I could learn much! Can this be arranged?"

"Well, I don't see why not," said Dad. "You seem to be a nice young man, and I think this would be interesting for everyone. Let's figure this out."

Mom served the coffee and cookies while Dad, Jim and Bubaka began working out the details. I wanted to put my two cents worth in, but Mom had warned Donna and me that we were to be quiet during this initial meeting. She did not want to offend Bubaka with the "forwardness" of American females, and we had both been assured of being sent to our room if we couldn't keep our mouths shut. I fidgeted and wiggled in my chair, but I did manage not to interrupt and blurt out my opinions.

It was finally agreed that Bubaka would come to our house once a week on Thursday evenings. Each week we would mutually pick a subject for discussion. Out of respect for American traditions, Mom, Donna and I would be allowed to attend the discussions and remain unveiled. Out of respect for Arabic traditions, we would keep a low profile and direct our comments or questions through Dad. The subject for the first meeting the following week was markets and shopping. When Bubaka left that night, he was extremely happy and grateful, and we were excited about this unique opportunity for us to learn so much about our temporary home.

The first few evenings we spent with Bubaka tended to be a bit stiff and awkward. Everyone was sort of "feeling their way" through the situation and wary of accidentally treading on cultural toes. Also, though Bubaka spoke English, it was very archaic English, which made it difficult to understand him. It was rather like being exposed to Chaucer or Shakespeare in the original language: you could tell that it was English, but it took a lot of concentration to decipher it.

Bubaka kept a small notebook and used it frequently. On his fourth visit, he asked if we could spend the evening answering some questions that he had. He then pulled out his notebook, and his questions were all about English usage. For example, he had been taught the old pronouns (thee, thou, etc.), but he noticed that we never used them, and he wanted to know why. When Bubaka left that evening, Jim told me to be sure to bring my English textbook home with me on Thursdays.

After that, on "English night" (about once a month) Jim and Bubaka would sit at the dining room table while Jim tutored him. My sixth-grade English text proved to be a valuable resource for clarifying verb conjugation, proper use of pronouns, modifying phrases, and so on. Bubaka was delighted, and "Jeem" had a natural flair as a teacher.

Several months passed in this way, and everyone gradually relaxed. We gained a wealth of information about Libya. Bubaka told us about two cities of Roman ruins on the Libyan coast, Sabratha and Leptis Magna. He told us how to find the Artisan's Courtyard in Tripoli, the fish market, and the best places to shop. We told him about life in America, and showed him our photo albums with pictures of our house and hometown. We spent one evening comparing the Koran and the Bible and found them surprisingly similar, at least until you got to the New Testament. Bubaka's English became more and more fluent and modern, and the actual tutoring sessions grew further apart and gradually ceased. The visits, however, continued.

*   *   *

Six months or more had passed since we first met Bubaka. School had ended for the year, we had gone through summer break, and school was again back in session. I was twelve and was now in junior high as a seventh grader. Donna was fifteen and a sophomore in high school, and Jim was in his senior year. By now, Bubaka had grown relaxed and comfortable around all of us.

On the evening in question, Mom and Dad had invited Bubaka to dinner with us, and that night's subject of discussion was marriage customs. We were all seated around the dining room table and talking over the meal. Bubaka had told us that in Libya, the parents of couples arranged marriages. Girls were married at a very young age—usually around twelve or thirteen, but the boys were a bit older, around sixteen or so. There was a bride price paid to the family of the girl, and in return the girl brought a dowry with her to the family of the groom. Usually, the couple being married didn't even meet one another until the day of the wedding.

In return, we tried to explain American dating: sock-hops at the school; getting a hamburger, fries and a shake before going to a movie; and going to football games. Bubaka simply could not absorb the concept, and was particularly shocked that such dates were not chaperoned. Trying to retain a little respectability, Dad explained that he insisted on meeting any young man that took out one of his daughters, and since we were from a small town he also knew the families and their reputation. Bubaka looked skeptical of the whole arrangement, and I don't think he really believed us. The conversation drifted into more general areas. For the rest of the meal, Bubaka seemed a bit distracted and thoughtful.

Finally, over dessert and coffee, Bubaka looked at Dad and hesitantly said, "My friend, I would like to ask you a question, but I don't want to give offense. It is something I am wondering about, but it is a very personal question."

"Oh, go ahead and ask me. If it's *too* personal, I'll let you know."

"Well, you have two daughters who are still living in your home."

Dad glanced at Donna and me, and said, "Yes, that's right."

"But it appears to me that they are both old enough to be married and living in the homes of their husbands. Why are they still in the home of their father?"

Dad sat back and looked at us again. The evening's discussion must have been running through his head and, thinking to make a joke, he said, "Well, to be honest with you, Bubaka, I haven't gotten a good enough offer yet and, of course, you have to marry off the older one first."

Bubaka's eyes widened as he looked at Dad and then quietly asked, "And for your older daughter, what would you consider to be a good offer?"

Dad looked Donna over and, still joking, said, "Oh, I don't know. Let's see … Maybe two camels and a donkey—that sounds about right."

Bubaka rose to his feet, bowed slightly to Dad, and said, "Please, you must excuse me." Then, before you could say "wedding invitations," he turned and hurried out the front door.

Dad looked around at us and said, "What? What did I say this time? Or do you think it was something he ate? Do you think he's sick?"

Jim replied quietly, "I'm not sure, Dad, but I think you may have just sold Donna to an Arab."

"*What?*" Donna shrieked as she leapt to her feet, nearly knocking her chair over backwards. "*My Dad sold me to an Arab? How could you do that!*" Then she turned and ran down the hall to our room.

I jumped up and was right behind her, shouting, "No! I won't let them do it! They're not going to take you away!" We raced into our bedroom together, and slammed the door behind us. I grabbed the dresser and started dragging it in front of the door. "C'mon, Donna, we gotta block the door!" Together, we barricaded the door with every piece of loose furniture that we could move.

A few minutes later there was a light tap on our bedroom door, followed by Mom's voice. "Girls? Are you all right?"

"NO!" we both shouted together.

Mom tried the door handle and found that the door wouldn't move more than about an inch. "Now, come on, girls, you're being silly."

"*You let Dad sell me to an Arab! I'm never coming out of here again!*"

"Donna, I think it was just a misunderstanding. We'll work through this, and everything will be all right. Now, unblock this door, please."

"*No! I'm not going to risk it! I'm staying in here!*"

There was a pause, and then Mom said, "All right. You can stay in there for now, but you're going to have to come out sooner or later. Let's just see what happens." We could hear her footsteps as she walked back down the hall.

Donna and I sat on our beds talking, trying to figure out how we could run away and escape from a foreign country. We debated whether or not Dad's goofy comment could possibly be interpreted as a legally binding contract. We dragged out our suitcases and started packing our clothes.

About an hour later, there was knock at the front door. Bubaka had returned, and brought with him his father and his uncle. They also had with them a donkey, three goats, and several chickens. Dad opened the door and invited them in, but he insisted that the livestock be left outside. He assigned Massoud the job of keeping an eye on the animals so they wouldn't be lost or stolen.

I had opened our bedroom door the inch that it would move, and had my ear pressed to the crack. I could hear the murmur of voices, but I couldn't make out what was being said. Since Donna and I needed information, I decided to play spy. We eased the barricade back enough so that I could slip through the door. In my stocking feet, I crept back down the hall and pressed myself up against the wall of the living room near enough to the door so that I could hear but not be seen.

My worst fears were confirmed! Bubaka was there with his father and uncle to make a counter offer for Donna's bride price. Apparently, they didn't have two camels handy, so the barnyard assortment in the street outside was their offer. They were most interested in "sealing the deal" that night. Bubaka must have felt like he had hit the lottery—to get an American bride (which also meant American citizenship) for a donkey, some goats, and a few chickens was the deal of the century!

Dad tried to explain that he had been joking. Bubaka's family was not amused. Dad then said that selling one's children was illegal in the United States and there was no way that he could accept their animals in exchange for his daughter. They mulled that over, and asked what, exactly, would he accept as a bride price, which is something entirely different than selling. The discussion went back and forth, with Bubaka interpreting in the middle. Dad was getting more and more desperate for them to understand that Donna was not for sale. Bubaka's family was getting more and more irritated because Dad wouldn't stop waffling around and name a price that could be worked with.

By now, Donna had also crept out of our room and was pressed up against the wall beside me. We were almost ready to sneak back to our bedroom and escape out the window when we heard the soft murmur of Mom's voice. We couldn't make out what she was saying. Then we heard Dad sigh in relief. In very formal tones, he addressed Bubaka and his family.

"My wife tells me that she cannot possibly allow either of my daughters to be married yet. She says that it is entirely her fault, and she has been far too lax with them. She has not properly trained them in the duties of a wife or the management of a home—they do not know how to clean, care for children, or cook."

"I can too cook!" hissed Donna.

"Shut up, Stupid! You'll just get yourself in more trouble!" I hissed back.

In the living room, Dad continued, "Because of this, my wife says that she cannot allow the shame and embarrassment to me or to the groom's family of such a poorly prepared wife."

Bubaka translated all of that, and there was some more discussion between his father and uncle. Finally, Bubaka said, "My father understands now. He suggests to you that perhaps you should beat your wife more often to impress on her the duties of a mother. We are very sorry that we could not reach agreement, but he appreciates the honesty you have shown in admitting the serious faults of your daughters. We will leave now."

Donna and I scurried back around the corner and out of sight. The men in the living room stood up, shook hands all around, and bowed to one another. Then Bubaka and his family left, taking all of their livestock away with them.

*   *   *

Bubaka didn't show up the following Thursday night. Several weeks passed and he still did not return. We figured that the embarrassment and the insult of the situation had simply been too much for him to deal with. We missed our friend and all the interesting things that we had talked about. On the other hand, we were all relieved that we had scraped through a potential "international incident" with as little fallout as there was. We were also delighted that Donna, even though she was now a two-camel woman, was still at home, unmarried.

Then, at about five-thirty on a Thursday night in early December, there was a knock on the door. Dad answered the door to find Bubaka standing there, holding a large serving dish covered with a piece of embroidered linen. Bubaka bowed his head slightly and said, "My friend, I have returned. And, in celebration of the renewal of our friendship, I have brought dinner for all."

Dad was dumbfounded for a second, but he quickly recovered. Taking the dish from Bubaka, he said, "Well, this is wonderful. Welcome back! Come in, come in while I tell everyone." As Dad turned and led the way into the house, he called, "Bernice, come and see. Bubaka is here, and you don't have to cook dinner tonight."

Mom came into the front hallway, closely followed by us kids. She took the dish from Dad and said, "What a nice surprise this is. How very thoughtful of you, Bubaka. Thank you very much." She took the dish to the table and placed it, still covered, in the spot of honor directly in front of Dad's seat. Then she said, "Girls, I'll need help setting the table and, Jim, if you could come into the kitchen for a moment I have something I would like you to take to the living room." She said this quietly, but it was delivered in her "Mother's Voice of Steel" that brooked no argument or disobedience. The three of us quietly followed her to the kitchen.

In the kitchen, she turned and fixed all of us with one of her "Mother Looks." Then, in a low voice (so as not to be overheard in the living room) she said, "All right, we are all going to be very polite and gracious about this. I'm surprised that Bubaka even came back, and bringing dinner is like a peace offering. I will not have that young man insulted or embarrassed. So, no matter *what* is in that dish when the cover comes off, *that* is what we are having for dinner. You will each take some, and you *will* eat it. And, I will not tolerate any rude comments, noises, gagging, or throwing up. You don't have to take much, but you will eat it and behave as if you are enjoying it. Do I make myself clear?"

We nodded and murmured our assent.

Mom quickly assembled a tray with crackers, cheese, olives and fruit juice. Jim was dispatched to the living room with the appetizers while Donna and I set the table. When we were finished, Mom added her fancy candlesticks as a centerpiece, and a large basket of bread—Bubaka loved American bread and couldn't seem to get enough of it. When all was ready, Mom went to the living room and announced that dinner was served.

We assembled around the table and Dad led us in the Blessing Before Meals. Then, as we all leaned forward in anticipation, he ceremoniously removed the linen cover from the serving dish. It was a casserole type meal of spiced cous-cous with lamb and, proudly centered on top of it, were the lamb's eyeballs. For a few seconds Dad stared at the dish while the dish stared back at him.

This was an Arabic tradition we had all heard of. The eyes were considered a delicacy, and they were intended for the most important person at the meal. Since Dad was the "patriarch" of our family, that meant him. He gulped a little bit, and shot a frantic glance at Mom.

She surveyed the dish, then looked Dad right in the eye and said, "Leonard, what an honor for you. I'm sure you will enjoy them. Please, begin the meal."

Dad picked up the serving spoon and scooped the eyeballs onto his plate along with a bit of the cous-cous. While we all watched eagerly to see if he could actually *do* this, he used his fork to carefully lift the first eye. Taking a deep breath, he popped it in his mouth and swallowed it down. He was very pale, with a delicate green tinge that clashed with his red hair, but he bravely lifted the second eye. Taking a second, deeper breath and closing his eyes, he ate that one also. He sat still for a moment, then opened his eyes, forced a smile onto his face, and said to Bubaka, "Exquisite. You must give my compliments to the cook." Mom beamed at him from the other end of the table.

Bubaka replied, "Thank you, my friend. My mother will be both pleased and honored."

Dad then had us pass our plates and he served up dinner for everyone. The rest of the meal passed in animated discussion and laughter, and Bubaka consumed six pieces of bread with his cous-cous. Everyone was careful to avoid the subject of marriage traditions.

Bubaka continued to visit us regularly for the rest of our stay in Tripoli, and his friendship has remained a fond memory for all of us. Dad never again made the mistake of suggesting a bride price for either Donna or me, and we felt that his having to eat those eyeballs was more than enough vindication for the one time that he had.

"Orville Wright didn't have a pilot's license."

—Anonymous

By the Sea, By the Sea, By the Beautiful Sea

… as told by Donna

The Mediterranean Sea has to be the most beautiful, tranquil sea on this earth. That majestic body of water graces the entire north coast of Africa. The beaches are covered with fine white sand that gradually slopes out into the sea—no sudden drop-offs. The water near the shore is aquamarine colored, and the further you go out, it turns to a deep royal blue. Even at chest level, you can look down through the water and see your toes. When we were in Tripoli, it was frequently referred to as the "African Riviera."

The coastline around Tripoli was not developed with hotels, casinos, fancy restaurants, or other tourist attractions. It was in its natural state and sparsely populated. When we went swimming, we had the whole beach to ourselves. It was great!

We normally went swimming on Sunday afternoons. It was not a matter of throwing on ones' swimsuits and jumping into the car; it had to be *planned*. Preparations took at least an hour before we were ready to leave.

Mom would put together a substantial picnic lunch and make two large thermos jugs of Kool-Aid™, as well as a large jug of water. Dad would gather up blankets, a large tarp, poles, tools he would need to put up the tarp, flashlights, air mattresses and three rather large inner tubes. Believe it or not, all that "stuff" fit in the trunk of that old car of ours.

Then Mom would have to tend to us. She made sure we had beach towels, sandals, sun tan lotion, cover-ups in case we started getting sun burned, hats, and sun glasses. She would pack Raymond's little tote bag which contained his sand bucket, shovel and an assortment of other toys. In a separate cardboard box, she put a first aid kit, a snake bite kit, hairbrushes and combs, and calamine lotion.

None of us knew how to swim, not even Mom and Dad—not too smart for a family who planned to spend a day on a sparsely populated beach. I suppose our parents thought it was okay, keeping in mind the gradual slope of the beach into the sea and the calmness of the water. Jim and I decided, though, to teach ourselves how to swim just in case. We quickly found out that it involved more than just jumping in the water and splashing your arms and legs. So, Jim researched matter and came up with a sequence of actions that would guarantee to make us swimmers. All in all, it made a great deal of sense, was a lot of fun and would take us about ten summers to reach our goal. In spite of the odds, we went at our lessons with a great deal of vigor. Besides, it was a good excuse to nag Mom and Dad to make a trip to the beach every weekend, weather permitting.

Now, picture this: Dad would park the car right on the sand as close to the water line as he could without getting stuck. We would all pile out and grab whatever we were assigned to remove from the trunk, and begin to assemble or prepare the task we were responsible for. Dad immediately started attaching the tarp to the doors on one side of the car and securing them to five-foot poles, thus creating a shaded area for us when we needed a break from the blazing African sun. Jim and I had to blow up the air mattresses and retrieve the inner tubes (which were already inflated). Pat helped Mom lay out the blankets and the food items under the tarp. Emergency items were left in the trunk until they were needed (God forbid). We were also responsible for our own personal items, like our towels, sunglasses, hats, etc. I have no idea what Raymond was doing while all this activity occurred, but he never wandered off on his own. You could glance around at any time, and there he would be, standing in the same spot Mom put him when we exited the car.

When all of that was done, Jim, Pat, and I would strip off our clothes (we had our swimsuits on underneath them), grab something that floated, and run yelling towards the water. At the shoreline, we struck the water without a break in our stride and plunged into that beautiful sea. The temperature of the water was always mild—not screaming cold like the oceans—and a delight to our already slightly over-heated bodies. That was one of the biggest perks of being in Libya.

*   *   *

There were coral reefs situated about 100 yards off shore. These reefs had breaks in them that formed perfect alcoves in the area between them and shore. Dad had found a perfect cove in which we could safely play and "swim." He called it our "spot," and as many times as we went there, we had the entire beach to ourselves. Occasionally an Arab would come by with his donkey or mule to gather seaweed and to watch the crazy Americans risk their lives in the water, but that was all.

Some of the coral reef spread sparsely towards shore in the more shallow areas. Jim and I would flop facedown across an air mattress, have on our goggles with a snorkel attached, and investigate the coral life. That was definitely not something we could have done in Illinois. It was a live biology lesson, and we were always amazed and delighted at what we could see. The only marine hazards in our cove were moray eels. Sometimes they would come close to shore looking for food, especially if the sea was very choppy past the reef. If one was spotted, the person who saw it would yell "*eel, eel*" several times until everyone got out of the water. The rule was that we had to wait about a half-hour before we could go back in the sea. Don't ask me why it was a half-hour. All I know is that by that time they would be gone. You don't suppose it was all the hollering that could have made them leave?

*   *   *

One beautiful Sunday afternoon, after we had consumed our lunch and rested the mandated time before re-entering water, Jim, Pat, and I went out for the last two hours of the afternoon. Each of us had grabbed an inner tube, and was lazily floating around on the top of the water. If any one of us started drifting too far out, all we had to do was kick our feet and paddle with our arms and we would be back to the shore in a matter of minutes.

I had a full tummy, the warm sun was shining comfortably down upon me, and I was very relaxed. I fell asleep!

Someone calling my name over and over awoke me. I looked up from my inner tube and saw Mom and Dad waving at me from the shore. I smiled and waved back. They kept yelling my name, and added a great deal of back and forth arm-waving to their antics. I was confused and still a little sleepy. Then out of nowhere a *very* large wave hit me broadside with the force of a pickup truck. In seconds I was engulfed in seawater even though I was actually riding the top of the wave. I broke the surface, and was immediately plunged to the bottom of the wave's trough. The undertow dragged me further out.

It started to dawn on me how very far out I had drifted. Mom and Dad were these smaller than usual figures on the shore. Jim had joined them as well, and all three of them were yelling for me to try and come back in. I began furiously kicking my feet and paddling my arms. I would make a little headway, and, *bam!*, I would be hit by another monster wave and would be dragged backwards again. This voice in my head started saying, "You're going to drown, idiot. Keep kicking, keep kicking! Hurry up, you don't have a lot of time."

I had a brief glimpse of my mother entering the water. What was she doing? She couldn't swim. And then Jim followed her. I saw my Dad run towards the car for some reason. It was all frantic and quite scary. Was my fate to be to drown in the Mediterranean Sea?

Suddenly, everything went into slow motion. I was still paddling and kicking, the waves were still hitting me one after the other, and I was choking on mouthfuls of salt water. Through all that, I clearly saw my mother coming towards me. She would go down under the water, toe-step on the bottom, and then bounce up to get a lung-full of air. She did that over and over again until I felt her right hand touch my arm, and her left hand grab the inner tube.

"Keep kicking, Sweetheart, and I'll kick too. Don't move your arms, just hang on, and I'll do the paddling."

Together we struggled as hard as we could. Before I knew it I could reach bottom with my own toes. Jim was there, waiting to help Mom to shore, and Dad grabbed me up and out of the water. Pat and Ray were on the shore yelling my name while jumping up and down in celebration.

Both Mom and I were more than exhausted. We lay on the blanket under Dad's tarp, not moving for a long time. I softly told my mother "thank you" and that I loved her more than several times. She had saved the life she had given me 15 years earlier.

*   *   *

Needless to say, several lessons were learned that day, and some of the rules changed. My parents had been scared to their cores for me, but they did not forbid future trips to the beach. (They knew how much we loved our time spent there.) Instead, they tightened up the security measures.

Mom bought a big, noisy whistle that—I swear—could be heard in downtown Cairo, Egypt. One blow on that whistle meant someone was getting too far out, and *everyone* had to move closer to the shore immediately. Two blows on the whistle meant we had gotten too reckless and/or ignored the first whistle blow. Then *everyone* had to come out of the water and take a 10-minute shore break. Three blows on the whistle meant we had screwed up, and we all had to get ready to go home.

Dad made anchors for the air mattresses and the inner tubes. They were simple, but effective. He had punched a hole in a sealed strip of the tire or plastic mattress, attached a sturdy length of rope, and wound that several times around a large rock. When you plunked that thing into the water, it rapidly sunk to the bottom and embedded itself inches into the sand. No drifting allowed.

My drowning adventure was, from that time on, referred to as "Donna's tubing trip to Italy."

"If you always tell the truth, you can keep track of your stories."

—Bernice DeMuth

Beach Party

... as told by Donna

We had the afternoon off from school. Well, *technically* we didn't have the afternoon off; the school was having a large afternoon assembly for both the high school and the junior high school students. It would take the entire rest of the day.

We had less than a month left of the school year, so the administration planned one three-hour-long assembly to announce critical matters that would affect the up-coming school year. Things like athletic awards and new team captains, the newly elected cheerleaders for next year, the new members of the school choir, and the new members being inducted into the thespian club. In addition (and the highlight of the assembly), they would announce the winners of scholarships and the new inductees into The National Honor Society.

Since I was not a/an winner/inductee/member of any of the above mentioned groups, none of these events concerned me. Instead the day offered a bold, but workable, opportunity to do something I had never done before: skip school!

Bobbie and Sharon (my two best friends) and I had discussed this in the past. When we heard about the up-coming assembly, we excitedly began planning our adventure. Bobbie's boyfriend, Rob, had a car. We could meet him and my boyfriend, Paul, outside the cafeteria after the lunch hour. We would be wearing our bathing suits under our school clothes, and have towels stuffed into our book bags. The guys said they would buy some sodas and ice to put in Rob's cooler, as well as bring along a portable radio and some beach blankets. We had all our bases covered.

The day before the assembly, Sharon chickened out. She wasn't currently "going" with anyone and felt like she would be a fifth wheel. (In fact, at the

111

time, she had a raging crush on my older brother, Jim, which was hopeless. He said it wasn't advisable for him to date one of my best friends, in case things didn't work out.) Sharon also said that, for some reason, she had an uneasy feeling about skipping school that day, and wanted to play it safe. Bobbie and I gave her a little grief about her decision, but quickly backed off when we saw she was serious about her reasons.

I will admit that I too had a little nagging feeling about skipping school. I attributed it to the fact that this was my first time, and I didn't want to get caught. I wasn't remotely worried about missing out on the school announcements. Mom had teased me a little about accepting a nomination to The National Honor Society, and that I needed to wear one of my "prettier" dresses to school that day, so I looked especially good when I walked up onto the stage. I huffed at her comment, and told her that wasn't even remotely funny. She apologized for teasing me, but also added that I needed to have more confidence in myself.

Have confidence in what? Everyone in our family knew that I was not a scholar. That was Pat and Jim's role. They made straight A's throughout their school years. It wasn't human! And, to make things worst, they would get their text books the beginning of the semester, read them from cover-to-cover in one week, and never open them again except for a quick refreshing before a test. When report card time came around, Dad would get two rolls of dimes (the pay-off for an A) and one roll of nickels. (Guess who the nickels were for?) No matter how hard I studied, there was at least one (or more) subject that I got less than an A in.

During the school year, Pat and Jim rarely had to do homework (they would do it all in study hall). I didn't work that fast. So, night after night I would be segregated in my room, my nose in my books working my little brain to death. I would complain to Mom that it just wasn't fair. Why didn't my brain work the way theirs did? I was convinced without a doubt that I was retarded. Mother would chastise my attitude, and try to smooth me over by telling me that, "Pat and Jim were blessed with exceptional minds and memories, but God did not forget about you. He gave you a wonderful personality that outshines your brother and sister." Great! I was the designated retarded clown in the family.

Anyway, I did manage to lay aside my nervousness about skipping school, and decided to proceed with my plans.

*　　　*　　　*

It was an absolutely gorgeous day to go to the beach. It could not have been more perfect—the escape from school went flawlessly, and the rest of the day flew by quickly. All four of us had a great time.

We had timed it so we got back to the base in time to change back into our school clothes, and to catch one of the three buses going into Tripoli in the afternoon—business as usual. I was feeling very smug with myself for having successfully followed through with my caper.

*　　　*　　　*

I was energetically walking towards the bus stop when I heard my name being frantically called again and again. I stopped and looked behind me. Pat was running down the sidewalk towards me, waving her arms and yelling my name. I waited for her to catch up with me. She could hardly get her breath, and I couldn't make out what she was saying between her gasps for air.

I grabbed her shoulders to steady her, and said, "Whoa, slow down. I can't understand what you are saying. You're acting like it's the end of the world."

"It is the end of the world!" she declared. "Your end of the world!"

"What are you talking about?"

"You can't go home, Donna. If you do, they will murderize you. You gotta run away—get out of the country."

"Who's going to 'murderize' me, and why?"

"Mom and Dad. They know you skipped school today. They don't know where you were, but they do know you weren't in school. They said you'd show up sometime, and they would deal with you then. Your only chance to live is to run. Maybe you can go out to the big hangar, and stow away on one of the planes going to Rome. When you get there, catch a bus to the Vatican and go directly to St. Peter's Cathedral. Ask them for 'sanctuary' just like Esmeralda did in the *Hunchback of Notre Dame*. When things calm down, maybe you could get a job in a pizza parlor until you earn enough money to come back home. Where were you, anyway?"

"I went to the beach with Bobbie and Rob and Paul."

"Oh, boy, it's going to be worst than I thought. You'd better come up with a better story than that, if you want to live. I still think running away is the best idea."

After recovering my composure, I asked Pat, "How did they find out I skipped school?"

"They were at the assembly!"

"What? Why were Mom and Dad at the assembly?"

"They knew in advance that you were going to be inducted into The National Honor Society. They wanted to surprise you. Dad was up near the stage with his camera set up to take all kinds of pictures when they called your name. He was about to burst he was so proud. You shoulda seen the look on his face when he realized you weren't there. He walked back to his seat with his head down, and he wouldn't look at anybody. And, Mom made a cake and all for you that's waiting at the house. After the assembly, Jim caught me outside the hall, and told me to find you and let you know what happened. He was going to talk to Mom and Dad. Boy oh boy, what a mess! Ya' really screwed up this time."

I was in mild shock, and couldn't speak for a few minutes. When I could, all I could say in disbelief was, "I was inducted into The National Honor Society?"

"Yeah, you were, dummy. But you can bet your life you won't be a member come tomorrow."

Without taking a breath, Pat continued, "What time is it? I gotta go if I'm going to ride home with Dad." With that said she took off running down the sidewalk, but stopped half way down the block. She turned around and ran back to me. Unexpectedly, she grabbed me in a big bear hug and cried in my ear, "I'm gonna miss you a lot! Please write and let me know how you are." Then she was off again.

*   *   *

This was not the time to panic, so I walked down the sidewalk to the bus stop. I sat on the bench in the bus waiting area. No one else was there. I was numb, but I needed to think. My brain wouldn't work.

I took several deep breaths while staring up at the beautiful blue sky, and tried to sort things out.

Well, to start with, I couldn't run away to Rome as Pat suggested. I needed a safe place of haven, but nothing came to mind. What could I tell them? I could never convince them that I had gotten sick; besides I hadn't signed in at the school nurse's office. I could tell them Bobbie got sick and I had to stay with her. Would they believe me? Probably not, and knowing Mom and Dad they would check with Bobbie's mom.

Dozens of scenarios ran around my head, but they got more and more unbelievable as time went by. This little voice said in my ear, "*Why don't you just tell them the truth?*" Ye Gads! I'd probably end up in the Mediterranean Sea, but this time it would be sans inner tube.

The little voice spoke up again, "You are being very silly. When have your parents ever tried to kill one of their kids? Furthermore, when was the last time they even hit you? It's not them you can't face; it's what you did that you can't face. Now, get up and catch the bus, and go home and face the music, coward."

For one brief moment I wondered when the next plane to Rome was taking off. Then I gathered my resolve, and got on the bus that showed up about five minutes later.

*   *   *

Mom and Dad's car was parked outside the house, so I knew they were home. When I entered the house, it was dead silent inside. No cheery congratulation awaited me. I went into the kitchen first—it was empty. With a mental drum roll, I proceeded to the living room. Dad was in there sitting by himself.

"Hi, I'm home," I said.

"I can see that," Dad said. "Did you have a good day?"

"Kinda."

"I didn't. In fact, this has been one of the most humiliating, disappointing days I have had in a long time. How could you do this to me?"

"Daddy, I'm really sorry. I had no idea I was going to be inducted into the National Honor Society, and I didn't want to sit through three hours of that assembly."

"That is not an acceptable answer, young lady."

I didn't respond, but just stood there looking down at the floor.

"Your mother occasionally accuses me about you being my favorite child. You know what, she's right. (I gasped) I love you because you are *not* perfect, and have to work hard for what you gain in life, just like I did when I was your age. But one thing for sure is that you have never let me down until today. Do you have any idea how proud I was about your induction into the National Honor Society? Even though you didn't believe it, I did! Today, for the first time in your life, you broke my heart." (I looked up—there were tears in his eyes.)

My eyes started to tear too. "Oh, Daddy, I am so very sorry. I didn't think this would happen."

"That's exactly right. You didn't think! Because of your careless disregard, mixed with your lack of confidence, you have hurt every member of this family.

"I'm sorry," I said again, in a low whisper.

Dad paused, and then continued, "Contrary to what your sister may think, your mother and I are not going to kill you, but you will make this right. These are the things we expect you to do, with no whining or protesting: You will separately apologize to everyone in this family; when you go into school tomorrow morning, you will go directly to the principal's office and tell him what you did. You will take whatever punishment he assigns you. You are grounded for two weeks. In addition, your mother has prepared a special dinner for you and baked your favorite cake. You can have dinner, of course, but you will not eat a piece of that cake."

(I started to speak, and Dad stopped me.) "I am not finished yet, but you need to follow me first." He went into the kitchen and he opened the refrigerator door. He took out a bottle of pink champagne that was cooling there. (I really liked pink champagne.) He walked to the sink, uncorked the bottle and poured it down the drain.

*   *   *

The next morning I went directly to the principal's office before school started. It wasn't as bad as I thought it would be. I believe that it was the first time in the principal's career that a teenage student confessed a misdeed before he knew about it. For a few minutes he was speechless. I wasn't kicked out of the National Honor Society. He said that honor was based on academic achievement which I had earned and not on "social errors." I had to go to detention for one hour after school every day for one week. That was it! The principal also said that my honesty was commendable. (Bam! My conscience was hit directly in the solar plexus with that comment.)

I never came to see myself as a scholar. I still had to work very hard for my grades, and graduated with only a 3.7 grade point average. Years later, in our adult life, Pat and I both attended the American Airlines Academy to be certified in SABRE (the airline's very large and complicated software system).

There were a total of 600 points that a participant could earn on the tests throughout the course (to date only one person had earned all 600 points throughout the academy's history). Upon completion of the course, the trainer called each and every one of us into her office to give us our final results. Guess what? You got it. Pat earned all 600 points! I earned 598 points. When I was called into the trainer's office, she said:

"Donna, I know you and your sister were competing for the 600 points. You are not to be disappointed. Pat is an extremely smart learner, but, I must say, of the two, you have the most enjoyable personality."

"A-a-a-a-gh!"

"When traveling, you stay quietly in your assigned seat. It's simple courtesy to the other passengers."

—Bernice DeMuth

Westward Bound

… as told by Pat

It was early May, 1961, and it was time for us to leave Tripoli and go home. Because Jim had graduated from high school and would be attending college in the fall, our family had been given permission to return home early. Dad would be staying in Tripoli to finish his tour of duty, and he would be following us home in February.

The big MATS (Military Air Transport Service, commonly referred to on base as May Arrive on Time Service) plane was pulled up on the flight line and had a ground crew swarming over it in preparation for take-off. We had already turned in our Wheelus military ID's, had our luggage checked by both Libyan and American officials, and our passports had all the proper stamps, seals, stickers, initials, and signatures to allow us to leave Libya and re-enter the United States. We were now in the "terminal" (a room partitioned off inside one of the hangars) and waiting for permission to board. Dad had accompanied us through all the steps, and now he and Mom were sitting together and talking quietly while we waited.

My best friend, Tina, had come to see me off and we were clinging to each other, crying and hugging our way through the over-emotional farewells of which only teenage girls seem to be capable. We repeatedly promised to write to each other faithfully, reminded ourselves of the many fun times we had together, and mentioned vague plans for getting together again after we were grown up. Donna was going through a similar farewell with her best friends, Bobbie and Sharon, while Jim kept track of our little brother, Ray. Outside, the ground crew rolled a set of metal stairs up to the side of the plane, and then one of them was dispatched to the terminal to announce that it was time to begin boarding.

There were hugs and good-byes all around, and then Mom checked that we each had the carry-on luggage for which we were responsible. Finally, she and Dad hugged tightly and kissed goodbye. Then Mom herded us out the door and towards the plane. At the foot of the stairs I paused for a final wave to Dad and to Tina before I climbed up to the plane.

We found seats by the wings: Mom, Raymond and I were on one side of the aisle and Donna and Jim were on the other. We stowed our carry-on bags, settled in, and fastened our seat belts. In very short order, all the passengers were boarded, the steps were pulled away, and the door of the plane was closed with a very solid "thunk" sound. Within minutes the pilot fired up the first engine, which was the inboard engine on the wing outside my window. The engine coughed, sputtered, and then caught with a roar as the big propeller began to spin. The other three engines were started in turn, first the inboard on the other side, then the outboard on my side, and finally the outboard on the other side. The entire plane was vibrating and shaking, and you had to yell to be heard over the engine roar.

Slowly, we trundled out to the end of the runway. We stopped there while the pilot pushed the engines to an even higher pitch. At the point when you thought the plane was going to shake itself to pieces, we started to roll forward, quickly gaining speed as we went. Finally, after a few tentative bumps and jumps, the big plane lifted from the runway and barely cleared the palm trees at the end. We kept climbing and soon the azure waters of the Mediterranean were beneath us. The pilot banked the plane until we were heading west, and then he leveled it out. We were on our way home!

Once we reached cruising altitude, the pilot cut back the power to the engines and the deafening roar settled into a loud, steady drone. I yawned a couple of times to get my ears to pop, and found that I *could* still hear if people spoke loudly.

The steward, a young airman wearing his khaki Air Force uniform, went to the front of the cabin, picked up a microphone, and began making his announcements. "Welcome aboard the MATS flight from Wheelus to Charleston, South Carolina. We are flying in a C-121, the military version of the Constellation, and our estimated air time will be seventeen hours. There will be two layovers for maintenance and refueling. Each layover is estimated at two hours, and they will be in the Azores and Bermuda. We will arrive in the Azores in about five hours, at which point you will be off-loaded and provided a meal before we continue. Between the Azores and Bermuda, you will be provided a boxed meal onboard. Our ETA for Charleston is 0600 hours, local time."

He paused for a moment while he picked up a bright orange life preserver and held it up so everyone could see it. Then he continued, "The majority of this flight will be over deep water. There is a life preserver located under each seat. If we should have to ditch over water, take the life preserver, pull it over your head and fasten the ties on the sides. To inflate it, you will pull the two valve stems located on the front. *Do not inflate your life preserver until after you exit the plane.* These are standard issue preservers, and are rated to keep a weight of 200 pounds afloat for a minimum of twenty-four hours. The emergency exits are on both sides of the plane, over the rear of the wings. When we ditch, the plane should stay afloat for a few minutes, which will give you time to make an *orderly* exit. Any questions?"

I would have been more comfortable if he hadn't made "ditching over the water" sound like it was a standard part of the flight plan. However, we had made the same flight (in reverse) two years before, and there had been no need to even look at our "Mae Wests." Feeling like a seasoned international traveler, I settled back in my seat and began reading the book I had brought to pass the time.

After about an hour or so, I gave up on the book. The steady vibration of the plane made it hard to keep the page in focus, and my eyes were starting to feel the strain. I tried talking with Mom for a little bit, but it was difficult to carry on a conversation when you had to yell to be heard. Besides, she was distracted and busy with trying to keep Ray occupied and quiet. I ended up just sitting back in my seat and letting myself doze off for a bit.

When I woke up, it was getting dark outside. The sky was a deep navy blue, and far ahead of the plane the clouds were painted in reds and golds from the sunset. Out of the corner of my eye, I thought I saw something flicker on the wing. I turned my attention to the wing and the two big engines. There it was again! I clearly saw a faint blue flicker of light around the housing of the outboard engine. I stared in fascination.

In minutes, my fascination turned to horror. That flickering blue aura around the engine was made of flame. It was the same color as the flame on a gas stove, and it streamed back from the engine housing and dissipated over the back of the wing. The flickers were getting closer together, and now were creating a veil of flame that lasted for several seconds each time before it faded.

I reached over and clutched at Mom's arm. "Mom. Hey, Mom! Look!"

Mom leaned forward a little and turned towards me, "Look at what, dear?"

"Look at the wing! We're on fire!"

Mom looked out the window for a few seconds, and I saw her eyes widen in surprise. Then she took a deep breath and said, "I'm sure everything is okay. That's probably just hot exhaust fumes, and we couldn't see them until it got dark. If there was a problem, I'm sure the pilot and crew would be aware of it."

"Well, if it's normal how come it's only one engine?"

"Pat, keep your voice down, and settle down. I don't want you starting a panic."

I "humphed" in reply, but now my entire attention was focused on that engine. I was sitting on the edge of my seat with my nose almost against the window. About fifteen minutes later, the engine was sporting a continual blue sheath highlighted now with flickers of yellow flame near the front by the propeller. We were also beginning to trail a thin stream of black smoke. I grabbed Mom's arm again as I frantically pointed out the window.

Mom took one look out the window, then quietly reached up and pressed the call button for the steward. The young airman quickly appeared at the side of her seat. She motioned for him to lean down, and spoke quietly but directly into his ear. He shot a quick glance out the window, then hurried off in the direction of the cockpit. A few minutes later, the outboard engine sputtered a few times, and turned off. The big propeller gradually slowed to a stop.

The steward reappeared at the front of the cabin and picked up his microphone once again. "If I could have your attention, please. Some of you may have noticed that the pilot has turned off the outboard engine on the port side of the plane. That engine has developed a small oil leak, and the pilot has cut it for safety's sake. There is no need to worry. The C-121 is an extremely reliable plane. The MATS Connie can fly with only two engines operational. We're a little more than an hour out from the Azores, and the ground crew will complete any needed repairs during our layover there. Thank you."

I wasn't sure if I believed him, but there was no question that the flames had stopped once the engine was cut. Mom appeared to be relieved, and since no one else on the plane seemed to be worried I decided that I could relax and trust to the wisdom of my elders.

We landed in the Azores without further incident. There were two buses waiting to transport us to the Officer's Club where we would have dinner and wait out the layover. The layover was longer than planned—it was almost three and a half hours before we were taken back to the plane. Shortly after that, we were in the air once more, headed across the width of the Atlantic on our way to Bermuda. I had watched closely as the engines were fired up, and I was regularly peeping out the window to check on the outboard engine. It seemed to be working fine.

We had been underway about two hours when the outboard engine started acting up again. It sputtered and popped, and within minutes it was again encased in a pale blue aura of flame. I pointed it out to Mom, she called the steward, and once again the pilot killed the engine. Since it was now late at night, Mom told me to settle down and go to sleep. Right! Here we were, six hours or more from Bermuda, over deep ocean with one dead engine, I didn't know how to swim, and she wanted me to go to *sleep?*

I wiggled around for a bit, trying to get comfortable. Then I got up and clambered over Ray and Mom so I could go to the bathroom. When I got back, I crawled back across them to my seat and then decided I was cold. I got up again, made my way to the aisle, and went to find the steward to see if I could get a pillow and a blanket. I returned with a postage stamp sized pillow and a blanket that would fit a baby's crib, crawled back to my seat, and tried to arrange myself. I reclined my seat back, but that didn't help for more than a few minutes so I brought it back up again. I twisted and turned, trying to get the pillow and blanket arranged. Finally, Mom had enough of me and sent me over to sit with Donna and Jim on the other side of the plane.

I demanded the window seat, threatening to get airsick if I couldn't see outside. Donna shifted over to the center seat. I crawled across Jim's long legs, stepped on Donna's toes, and finally settled into my seat. Since they were also trying to sleep, all of this didn't make me very popular. I tried to sit still, and soon found myself staring mindlessly out the window as the minutes ticked away. Someone dimmed the cabin lights, and the drone from the engines proved to be hypnotizing. I dozed off.

My eyes snapped open. The cabin was still dim and peaceful, but *something* had woken me up. I sat still, listening intently. Then I heard a sort of coughing, sputtering noise to my right—outside the plane on the wing. I looked out the window and saw that the inboard engine on *this* side of the plane was now sheathed in blue flame, and the propeller was slowing and jerking.

I looked around. Donna and Jim were sound asleep and, across the aisle, Mom was peacefully napping, too. I eased myself up from my seat and a quick scan of the cabin showed me that almost all of the other passengers were also asleep. There were a few reading lights on near the back of the cabin, but it was apparent to me that I was the only one on board who was aware of impending doom. I stretched my arm as far as I could and pressed the call button for the steward. Just as I pressed it, I lost my balance and fell across Donna and Jim's laps, abruptly waking both of them.

"What the hell?" growled Jim.

"*What* do you think you're doing?" Donna demanded, pushing at me to get me off her lap.

I was thrashing around, trying to push myself up and get my feet back under me, but succeeding in just getting my arms and legs more tangled up with Jim and Donna. In the middle of this Three Stooges scenario the steward appeared, demanding to know what was going on. He got a hold on my arm, and helped pull me to my feet. Donna, Jim, and the steward were all glaring at me.

I glared back at the steward and, with an air of wounded dignity, said, "Well, I'm *sorry*, but I thought you *might* like to know that we're on fire again." I turned and pointed in the direction of the window where the merry, flickering blue glow from the engine was clearly visible. The steward hurried off to the cockpit.

Mom immediately stepped into his place in the aisle and leaned towards me. "Patricia Jean!" she hissed. "You will sit down, shut up, and stay put! You have got to stop disturbing people! I do not want to hear another peep from you until we get to Bermuda!" She stepped back and returned to her seat, quickly checking that my little brother was still asleep. She shot me a final glare, then settled back, closed her eyes, and tried to go back to sleep.

Donna and Jim both gave me dirty looks and grumbled a bit before they, too, tried to go back to sleep. A glance out the window showed me that the pilot had killed the inboard engine on this wing. Now we were down to two engines, and Bermuda was still several hours ahead. I sat still in my seat, wide awake and concentrating hard as I mentally reviewed everything the steward had said when the flight started. I kept looking out the window, searching for even a hint of a blue flicker around the other engine.

I had just started to relax a little when we ran into turbulence. The plane shuddered and then plunged sickeningly downward. We lurched back up and slewed sideways. For a few minutes we bounced around like a pea in a blender, and soon most of the passengers were awake. Our ever-optimistic steward reappeared at the front of the cabin with his handy microphone at the ready. "Nothing to worry about, folks. We've run into a storm that's causing a little turbulence. The pilot's going to try to climb above it, but you might want to fasten your seat belts, just in case."

In case of what? I thought. The roar of the engines increased, and the cabin floor tilted slightly upward as we started to climb. Half an hour later we were still careening along through thick black clouds, rain was pounding on the windows and the fuselage, and huge forks of lightning were flashing around us outside. We had climbed slowly but steadily, but we still hadn't gotten out of or above the storm. The cabin floor leveled out and we lurched along through the turbulence.

Suddenly, a huge bolt of lightning sizzled down through the clouds right outside the window—it looked like it missed the tip of the wing by inches. It was instantly followed by a tremendous crack of thunder that could easily be heard over the engine noise. Without understanding how I got there, I was on my knees, scrabbling under the seat with my hands.

"What are you doing *now?*" demanded Donna. "Did you drop something?"

"No!" I snapped back.

"Then what are you doing on the floor, for heaven's sake?"

"I'm looking for that life preserver thing."

"Will you get back in your seat!"

I looked at my sister and said, "Look, he said this thing could fly with two engines. Well, in case you haven't noticed, that's what we're down to, and we're in the middle of a hurricane. If we're gonna 'ditch over deep water,' I'm gonna be ready!" I ducked my head down again, trying to peer under the seat.

Jim's hand clamped onto my shoulder, and he dragged me up off the floor and pushed me back into my seat. Still leaning across Donna he said, "Patty, you are acting like a total idiot. Yeah, the storm is scary, but we have to trust the crew. Now, you stay put in that seat, and stay quiet. Going crazy isn't going to help anybody." He reached across me and jerked the curtain closed over the window, blotting out the wing, the dead engine, and the wild night outside.

I sat bolt upright in my seat, every muscle tensed and my hands clamped on the ends of the armrests. Gradually, the turbulence let up, and we finally flew out of the storm. The steward announced that we were about an hour out from Bermuda, and then he distributed our box lunches. The meal consisted of a sandwich made with some kind of rubbery (and unidentifiable) cold cut meat, an apple, two very stale cookies, and a can of fruit drink. As a last meal for the condemned, I thought it left much to be desired.

When we touched down in Bermuda, I almost melted with relief. As we left the plane, the sky was just beginning to lighten with the impending dawn. The horizon to the east showed heavy clouds that were lit from below with a lurid red glow. We turned our backs on the dawn and boarded a bus to the NCO club, where we would wait out the layover.

This time, the layover stretched out to almost five hours before they finally took us back to the plane. We boarded and got settled in our seats. The pilot started firing up the engines one by one. When he got to the third engine, there was a problem. He quickly killed all the engines, and we were all asked to please leave the plane again. At the foot of the stairs, I looked back at the plane—there was oil splattered all over the wing and also in a huge arc up across the fuselage. They hurried us onto the buses and back to the NCO club.

An hour later, we were in the air again—*in the same plane!* South Carolina was only a few hours away, but I was convinced we would never make it. All through the flight I kept remembering Dad's war stories about planes coming in "on a wing and a prayer." We still had two wings, but I started praying, anyway. The miles slipped away behind us.

I don't know whether to credit my prayers or the competency of the Bermuda ground crew, or maybe a combination of the two, but we made it to Charleston, South Carolina, with no further alarms. Nothing blew up, caught fire, or fell off the plane, and the weather remained calm and pristine. We touched down on the runway almost seven hours behind schedule, but safe and sound with all life preservers still fastened under the seats. We gathered up our possessions and exited the plane.

Outside on the tarmac, Jim and Donna stepped to the side, got down on their knees, and kissed the pavement. Mom quickly admonished them, "Oh, for heaven's sake you two. Get up and stop being silly."

As they got back to their feet, Jim replied, "Sorry, Mom, but this is the good ol' U.S. of A. and I, for one, am glad to be back. Now, the first thing I want is a real hamburger, a big order of fries, and a huge chocolate shake." He grinned at Mom as he swept Ray up into the air and set him on his shoulders for the long walk to the terminal.

"If you run between the raindrops, you won't get wet."

—Bernice DeMuth

Pardon Me, Boys, Is This the Chattanooga Choo-Choo?

... as told by Pat

Our luggage was piled in an untidy heap at the end of the row of very uncomfortable metal folding chairs where we were sitting, waiting for Mom. We were in the Administration Building on the air base in Charleston, South Carolina, and Mom was in the Personnel Transportation Office. Jim had his long legs stretched out and the back of his head leaning against the wall, trying to doze. Donna sat next to me with Raymond on her lap and her arms loosely wrapped around him as he slept. I was sitting on the third chair, and I was developing a case of the fidgets. We had been waiting for almost an hour.

I nudged Donna and asked, "What's taking so long? Where's Mom?"

"They have to make arrangements to get us home. The plane from Tripoli was so late getting in that we missed our flight today. Mom's in there working everything out with them."

"But why is it taking so long?"

Jim tipped his head forward so he could see me and said, "Because it's the military. Have you ever known them to do something like this fast? There'll be a raft of forms to fill out, and dozens of signatures and stamps, and then they'll want at least four copies of everything. Just relax and wait. At least we have chairs to sit on."

With a dramatic groan, I settled back to wait some more.

Another twenty minutes ticked by before Mom finally came out of the office. She had a sheaf of papers in her hand, and even though she looked exhausted she was smiling as she sat down next to Jim. She took a deep breath and let it out slowly before she said, "All right. We've finally got everything worked out. We will be taking the train to get home."

Jim looked at her and asked, "The train? I thought we were supposed to fly?"

"No, not this time. It would take two different planes to get us to Chicago, and at this late date they couldn't find five open seats on anything that made sense. By taking the trains we'll be leaving this evening, and we'll actually get to Chicago at about the same time as if we flew. And, on the trains, we won't have to spend hours and hours sitting in airports."

"Sounds like we'll be spending them sitting in trains, instead," sighed Jim.

"No, no. We've got Pullman tickets all the way to Chicago so we'll have plenty of room and *beds* at night. We have one long layover tomorrow in Washington, DC, and then we don't change trains again until we get to Chicago. Now, just trust me that this will work out just fine."

"Okay, Mom. So, what's next?"

"First of all, I want you, Jim, to keep track of all these papers. These are our tickets, meal vouchers, and luggage ID's." She handed the stack of paper to Jim. "Now, we're supposed to go out to the bus stop in front of this building and catch a bus that will take us over to the Mess Hall, where we can all get a decent meal. After that, I'm supposed to call the Motor Pool, and they'll provide car service to take us all to the train station in town. So, if everyone is ready, let's get going."

With various moans and groans, we hauled ourselves to our feet and collected all of our luggage. We were all tired, having just spent more than twenty-four hours in the trip from Libya to Charleston with very little, if any, sleep. We were also dealing with an eight-hour time change and even though the afternoon sun was high in the sky, our bodies were telling us it was *really* late in the evening. The Mess Hall sounded good, though, because our last meal had been a military "box-lunch" handed out on the plane shortly before dawn and we were all ravenous.

When we arrived at the Mess Hall, we found that the building included a recreation room. The sergeant in charge told us to pile our luggage in the corner of the rec room and leave it there while we ate—he would keep an eye on it and it would save us the trouble of trying to manage our food trays along with the luggage.

To our delight, it turned out that the cooks could produce a respectable American hamburger and fries, as well as thick, creamy milkshakes. In Tripoli, milk was delivered to the base in powdered form and reconstituted with heavily chlorinated water. We had quickly learned to avoid milk and anything made with it. If you can imagine a bleach-flavored milkshake, you can understand why all four of us kids decided on a "real" milkshake to accompany our first American meal in two years. Mom ordered something sensible for herself, with lots of coffee.

While we ate, Mom explained our itinerary to us. We would leave Charleston that evening at eight o'clock on a train that would take us to Washington, DC. We would arrive in the capital at about 8:30 the next morning, and wouldn't leave there until 6:00 in the evening. In Washington, we would change trains and proceed to New York, and then across country to Chicago. That trip would take all night, the following day, and another night. We would arrive in Chicago mid-morning of the second day, when we would change train stations as well as trains and take the Illinois Central home. Since that train didn't stop in Paxton, she had already called Mr. Baier in our hometown, and he would meet our train in Rantoul and get us home. We had Pullman accommodations all the way, so all we would have to do is relax and enjoy the trip.

After the meal, we went to collect our luggage. To my teen-aged embarrassment, Mom did some quick rearranging and repacking right in the middle of the rec room. When she was done, we each had a small carry-on piece with personal things like toothbrushes, combs, deodorant, soap, etc. There was one large suitcase that had pajamas for everyone as well as fresh underwear and enough changes of clothes to get us through the trip. The other three suitcases and two duffel bags were closed and secured, and then we spent several minutes tagging everything. When everything was ready, Mom called the Motor Pool for our "car service" which turned out to be another bright blue Air Force bus. Though inelegant, it still proved to be efficient transportation to the train station.

On that train, we had a large room with a private bathroom and six berths. The berths were arranged in three groups of two, and they were similar to bunk beds—one on the bottom and the other one above it. Mom quickly got Raymond settled in a lower berth, and then claimed another one for herself. Since the lower berths were slightly larger, Jim claimed the third one because of his height. That left upper berths for Donna and me, a situation that didn't please either of us. I also saw fit to complain about having to share a bedroom with my *brothers*, but Mom was in no mood for any of it. In very short order, she had rotated us through the bathroom so we could clean up and change into our pajamas, gotten us into our berths, and turned out the lights. We were so exhausted that we were all asleep shortly after the train left the station.

*   *   *

The next morning we were all awake early. We again took turns in the bathroom, getting dressed and ready for the day. The luggage was repacked and piled near the door of our compartment. We were sitting on the bench-like seats and watching out the window as the train approached Washington.

"Well, all right," said Mom. "We'll be in the capital in about an hour, and then we have a very long layover. How do we want to spend the day?"

"You mean we don't have to wait in the train station?" asked Donna.

"I don't see why we should. Our train doesn't leave until six o'clock this evening, and train stations can be pretty boring," replied Mom.

"Where is the train station located?" asked Jim. "Is it close to anything interesting?"

"Well, I'm not sure, but I think the station is right in the heart of the District. We should be close to something worth seeing."

Jim perked up immediately. "I'd like to see the Smithsonian if we can, or maybe the capital building. I've heard you can sit in on sessions of Congress."

"What's the Smithsonian?" I asked.

"It's a big museum, and they have all kinds of stuff. They have the original *Spirit of St. Louis*, the plane that Lindbergh flew across the Atlantic."

Donna looked doubtful. "You mean they have his actual plane there, not just a model?"

"Yeah, it's the real plane. They've got a lot of other stuff about the history of the United States. And the Smithsonian is located on the quadrangle that has the Washington Monument at the end of it."

Mom added, "I would like to see The Library of Congress if we could fit it in. Tell you what, when we get in let's find someplace for breakfast and get a map. While we eat, we can check over the map and figure out what we can see. After all, we've got a whole day in the nation's capital, and we might not get this kind of chance again for a long time. Let's not waste it."

When we arrived at the station, Mom quickly found a porter and checked the bulk of our luggage through to Chicago. Next, we found a locker where, for a quarter, we could store our carry-on luggage for the day. Jim was given the job of keeping track of the key to the locker. Next, Mom bought a map of the District at a newsstand, and then we went to the diner in the station where we were allowed to order anything we wanted for breakfast.

While we were eating, Mom and Jim took turns poring over the map. They finally decided on going to the Smithsonian first, followed by the Washington Monument. From there we would go to the capital building and after that, if time allowed, we would visit The Library of Congress. Everything appeared to be within walking distance.

The Smithsonian was fascinating, though much bigger than any of us had thought it would be. We hadn't realized that it occupied several buildings. We picked out some areas that we wanted to explore, and spent most of the morning doing so. When we saw *The Spirit of St. Louis*, I was surprised at how small the plane was. Thinking about the trip across the Atlantic that we had just completed, I was amazed that Lindbergh had the courage to try the same thing all alone in that tiny plane.

From the Smithsonian we went to the Washington Monument where Jim, Donna and I decided we wanted to climb to the top. Jim was the only who made it all the way up; Donna and I pooped out about a third of the way up and had to sit on the stairs to catch our breath before we climbed back down. After that, we walked around the quadrangle and found a vendor with a hot dog cart. We had an impromptu picnic lunch while sitting on the grass of the quadrangle.

From the quadrangle we made our way to the capital building where we were, indeed, allowed into the gallery to observe Congress in session. A bill was under discussion, but there were no fiery arguments or brilliant orations going on. The discussion droned on for the fifteen minutes we were allowed in the gallery, and when we left I had decided that politics had to be the most boring job in the world.

The last thing on our list was The Library of Congress, and a guide told us that we could take the subway directly from the Capital to the Library. The "subway" turned out to be a long, subterranean tunnel with a "train" made up of something like six golf carts strung together. It was something you would expect to find in an amusement park rather than the nation's capital. However, the carts got us to The Library in short order, and we didn't have to walk (which was pleasant because we were all getting a bit tired).

I was disappointed to find out that we wouldn't be allowed to roam at will through the stacks of The Library of Congress. We spent about an hour looking at the displays in the main lobby area. One display that I remember was a cast taken of Abraham Lincoln's hands right after his inauguration. The right hand was swollen to almost half its size again, and the information placard said it was from all the handshaking that the President endured throughout the day. Gazing at that swollen hand, I decided once and for all that politics was not going to be one of my career choices.

By then it was late afternoon and time to return to the train station to continue our odyssey homeward. We were all pretty tired, but Mom had taken what could have been a boring, irritating day and turned it into a fun and informative field trip instead. For me, it reconfirmed that I had one of the smartest moms on the face of the earth.

*   *   *

At the train station we retrieved our carry-on luggage, checked in, and were directed out to the platform and the correct train. Mom went to the conductor and showed him our tickets, and he escorted us to the Pullman car. He helped us aboard and then took us to our compartments. While Raymond (not quite five years old) would be accommodated in Mom's compartment, the rest of us each had a private compartment all to ourselves. The conductor demonstrated how everything worked, where the call button was for the porter, and how to lower the bed. He turned a handle on the wall, and the entire wall folded down to become a very comfortable looking bed that filled the compartment. He then lifted the bed back up, pressed it flat and turned the handle, and it was once again the back wall of the compartment.

I was delighted. Even at home I didn't have a private bedroom but shared one with Donna, instead. When the bed was folded up, there was a comfortable couch-like seat next to a big window. There was a small tabletop that folded down from the side wall in case you chose to dine "en suite." There was even a private sink and toilet in the corner that also folded down for use and neatly folded away when you didn't need them. When the bed was opened the toilet and sink were inaccessible, so I asked what one did if one had to use the restroom in the middle of the night. Donna rolled her eyes at me, but the conductor graciously pointed out that there was also a public restroom at the end of the corridor. He then wished us a good trip and went back to his duties.

We each went into our own compartment to settle in and simply rest for a few minutes as we waited for the train to get started. Soon, I heard the conductor calling, "All-l-l-l abo-o-o-ard!" A few minutes later, the car shuddered, jerked, and began slowly rolling forward as the engine began moving us out of the station. We maintained a sedate pace as we passed through the congested areas of the city, but soon we were on more open track and began to pick up speed.

I decided it was time to explore my compartment, and to make sure everything worked the way the conductor had described. The first thing I wanted to see was the bed. I stood up, examined the handle in the wall, and then grasped it and gave it a hard pull to the left. Just as described, the wall released and began to fold outward, descending slowly to the horizontal. What hadn't been described was how heavy the whole thing was. I pushed hard against the wall, trying to slow or stop its descent, but I was fighting a losing battle. I couldn't get out from under it fast enough to get to the door, and I felt my knees start to buckle as the descending wall pressed me to the floor. I ended up on my hands and knees in a little cubby-hole in front of the seat.

I tried pushing up against the bed, but I couldn't budge it. The only thing left was to attempt an escape. With some judicious wriggling and scooting, I managed to get to the door leading into the corridor. It was a tight squeeze, but I finally managed to crawl into the corridor and stand up. From there, I tried lifting the bed once more, but it was hopeless—it appeared to be a case of an immovable object pitted against a more than resistible force. I went down the corridor and poked my head into Jim's compartment.

"Hey, Jim? I need some help"

"What's the problem?"

"Well, the bed in my compartment kinda came down, and I can't get it back up. Can you help me with it?"

"It just came down on its own?"

"Well, sort of. And it's really heavy and I can't get it back up."

Jim stood up and started towards me. "And all this happened without any help from you, right? The bed just mysteriously came down all on its own?"

"Well, I may have accidentally bumped the handle just a little. But the bed did come down and it kinda squashed me."

We were now at the door of my compartment. Jim slipped his hands under the edge of the bed and heaved it upwards. As it lifted he stepped into the compartment, firmly pushing the bed into place and latching the handle.

Jim looked at me and said, "Okay, it's fixed. When you're ready to go to bed let me know and I'll let it down again. Now, why don't you just sit quietly until it's time for dinner, and try not to break too many things. Mom, at least, will be upset if they throw you off the train." He turned on his heel and went back to his compartment.

I sat for about a minute, then got up and checked out the drop down table, the sink, and the toilet. I pushed the window shade up and down a few times, and I also found a small closet. I wanted to test the call button for the porter but decided against it. What would I do with a porter when one showed up? All in all, though, I was happy with my room and getting excited about spending the next forty hours or so on the train.

I heard Mom call me from her compartment across the hallway, and I hurried over to see what she wanted. When I poked my head through her door, she said, "Why don't you collect Jim and Donna, and we'll all go up to the dining car for dinner. How does that sound?" It sounded great to me, and I quickly rousted out my older brother and sister. Soon, the five of us were making our way up the corridor to the end of the car.

Jim opened the door and we were confronted with the space between the two cars. The car in front of us was rocking along, but it wasn't rocking in synchronization with ours. There was a metal plate that covered the coupling, but the plate was also moving and shifting around. We would have to cross it to get to the next car.

"This is really quite safe," Mom said encouragingly. "Just focus on the next car and step quickly across the plate. It's somewhat like stepping onto the first step of an escalator. You just need to be careful and sure of your footing."

Jim studied the path across the coupling for a few seconds, and then he reached down and picked up Raymond. Holding Ray securely, he stepped quickly and confidently across to the next car. Donna followed right behind him. It took me several false starts before I could finally place my foot on that shifting plate and from there practically leap to the next car. Mom followed me, patted me on the shoulder, and told me I had handled it like a pro. The dining car was four cars up the train, so we had to repeat the performance three more times to get where we going.

The waiter seated us at a large table by a window and handed us our menus. I was surprised—it was like eating in a fancy restaurant. We had a very nice meal, and talked about our day in Washington and all the things we had seen. Outside, the twilit countryside flowed past as the wheels clacked rhythmically beneath the car. I was beginning to appreciate Mom's attitude about trains—this sure beat the box lunch we had been given on the plane.

The waiter happily and politely accepted some of our military meal vouchers as payment for our dinner, and Mom left him a tip slipped discreetly under the edge of her saucer. We got up and started back to the Pullman car. While none of us were looking forward to crossing four couplings, at least we felt more confident about doing so.

It was at the last coupling that disaster struck. As usual, Mom made sure that we were all safely across before she followed. Just as she started to step over the coupling, the train jerked hard. She lost her balance for a moment, and shortened her step to compensate. Her foot came down between the edge of the car floor and the edge of that nasty, shifting plate as the cars jerked again. She let out a little yelp as her foot was pinned between the two pieces of metal. Jim instantly jumped back over the coupling, put his arms around her, and pulled her back as the plate shifted again, freeing her foot.

He held her steady for a few seconds while she caught her breath, and then anxiously asked her, "Mom? Are you all right? Can you put any weight on it?"

"I ... I don't know, Jim. It *does* hurt." Gingerly, she put her foot down and eased her weight onto it. With a gasp and a grimace of pain, she quickly stopped. "Oh, dear, I don't think I can walk on this, at least not right now. What will we do?"

"The first thing we do is get you into your compartment," replied Jim. "Okay, lean on me and I'll help you across. Ready? Okay, *now!*" We watched in surprise as our brother lifted Mom across the coupling, and then gently helped her into the Pullman car and back to her compartment.

He got her seated and made her put her foot up on the seat before he eased her shoe off her foot. Dark purple bruises were already blossoming across her instep. Jim reached over and pressed the call button for the porter. We were all crowded into Mom's compartment while we waited for the porter to arrive. Ray was whimpering a little, wide-eyed with fright and shock, and Donna was cuddling him and talking to him quietly, reassuring him that everything would be all right. Jim was gently examining Mom's foot, asking her if she could move it, where it hurt the worst, and so forth. I was nervously shifting from foot to foot, wanting to help and wishing someone would give me a task to do. Mom was very pale, but bravely trying to smile at us and forestall panic as she quietly answered Jim's questions.

When the porter arrived, Jim quickly and succinctly explained what had happened and asked for help. The porter took one quick glance at Mom's foot, told us all to stay put, and said he would be right back. He hurried off down the corridor.

He returned a few minutes later with a second man in tow, who was carrying a traditional black doctor's bag. The man stepped into the compartment and said, "My name is Dr. Thomas. The porter tells me there's been an accident?"

Jim replied, "Yes, our mother got her foot caught in the coupling thing when we were crossing between cars. I'm afraid it might be broken."

The doctor shooed Jim aside and took his place on the seat next to Mom. As he began examining her foot, he kept up a steady conversation with her, asking her name, about our trip, and exactly how her foot had been pinched. Then he moved on to the "does this hurt?" and "what about now?" as he manipulated her foot. Finally, he sat back and said, "All right, Mrs. DeMuth, you have a badly bruised foot and sprained ankle. I'm not feeling an obvious break, but you may have cracked one or more of the long bones through the instep, but that's impossible to tell without x-rays. The best we can do for now is to wrap this, keep it elevated, keep ice on it, and you should try to avoid standing or walking on it as much as possible. I can give you some pills for pain, and when you get home you need to have your own doctor take a look at this." He reached into his black bag and produced an Ace bandage.

The doctor had Jim and Donna watch as he carefully wrapped Mom's foot and ankle. He warned us to check the wrapping frequently because of swelling, and to loosen it if it became too tight. He dug around in his bag some more, and produced a bottle of pills, carefully counted out several that he slipped into a small envelope and gave to Mom with instructions on how often to take them. He suggested that she take one right then and, as if by magic, the porter produced a glass of water as well as a large, old-fashioned ice pack.

As the doctor stood up and collected his bag Mom said, "Thank you so much, Dr. Thomas. It already feels better just being wrapped. What do I owe you?"

The doctor looked back at her and replied, "Just follow my instructions and get to feeling better. I'm certainly not going to charge a soldier's wife for an Ace bandage and a few pills." He gave her a friendly smile as he left the compartment.

The porter reappeared, this time carrying a footstool and a couple of pillows. He arranged the footstool in front of Mom and, with a pillow on top of it, it was the perfect height for her to rest her foot on it without having to sit sideways on the seat. The porter tucked another pillow behind her neck and shoulders as she leaned back and relaxed. Finally, he arranged the ice pack so it covered her foot and ankle, and told us that when the ice melted we could get more from the club car. That sounded like a great job, and I immediately decided to become the ice monitor for the rest of the trip.

The pill was starting to take effect, and Mom looked at us sleepily and said, "Thank you all for being so helpful, and I am so sorry that this silly accident has interfered with our trip. But, if you don't mind, I think I would just like to rest for a little bit."

Donna replied quickly, "Of course, Mom, don't worry about anything. I'll take Raymond with me to my room, okay?" She collected a few of Ray's coloring books and the box of crayons before she guided him into the corridor.

"We'll leave your door open," added Jim, "and if you need anything at all either call us or use the button for the porter. I'll check back later and get your bed down for you." He switched off the overhead light, leaving the room softly lit by a small wall sconce. Then he turned and herded me into the corridor in front of him.

We reconvened in Donna's compartment, and Jim immediately took charge of the situation. "Well," he said, "this is an unexpected problem, but we're going to need to deal with it. Luckily, the doctor didn't seem to think anything was broken, and we've got a day and two nights before Mom is going to need to be getting around on that foot. She's going to go all stoic on us and pretend that it doesn't hurt, but if she uses that foot too much it's going to swell up and get worse."

"It seems to me," said Donna, "that we need to keep her pretty well settled and undisturbed in her compartment. What about meals? I can't really see her hopping over those couplings to get to the dining car."

"I'll talk to the conductor in the morning," replied Jim. "I'll see if they can't bring her meals to her compartment, and if there's an extra charge for that. Those pills will probably keep her pretty sleepy, but when she's awake I think we should take turns keeping her company.

I volunteered, "I can get ice for that ice pack—the porter said to just go to the club car and ask for it."

"And I can keep Raymond with me," added Donna. "What do you say, Raymie? Do you want to stay in here with me?"

Raymond thought about it for a few seconds and said, "Okay, but I still want to sleep in Mom's room." His big brown eyes reflected the fear and concern he was feeling, and Donna realized this request was more for reassurance than for anything else.

"That'll probably be okay, but we'll check with Mom about it. But during the day if she's sleeping or something, you can stay with us. Okay?"

"Okay. Is Mom going to be all right?"

"Sure she is. This is just a little accident, but she'll be fine."

"All right," said Jim. "Let's just all work together and take care of this."

*   *   *

For the rest of the trip, the four of us turned into what Jim called "Florence Nightingale Cadets." He coordinated things, took care of handling our vouchers and money when paying for things, and worked with the conductor and the porter so that Mom could have her meals in her room. He also became the designated person for putting beds up and down in the compartments.

Donna kept a close eye on Ray, keeping him busy during the day. She assigned Ray the job of pushing the button for the porter, a responsibility that Ray took very seriously and thoroughly enjoyed. She checked on Mom regularly and helped her with "personal" things like getting dressed, and she adjusted the Ace bandage a few times to keep a balance between swelling and circulation.

I made several trips to the club car to retrieve ice—as soon as Mom's ice pack showed signs of getting sloshy I was off to refill it. Mom was probably lucky that her foot didn't get frostbitten from my attentions. I also fluffed and rearranged pillows as needed.

The porter quickly turned into a valuable friend. He helped us with Mom's meal trays—he was very adept at crossing the couplings between cars—and checked on her several times during the day. With her permission, he gave Ray a guided tour of the train. Ray returned from that foray excited and chattering, and then spent a happy half-hour telling Mom all about everything he had seen.

By evening of the second day Mom was beginning to get up and move around a bit. Her foot was still tender and painful and she walked with a definite limp, but she was able to walk short distances. She wasn't going to win any races on that foot for awhile, but at least she could move around without severe pain. Dr. Thomas had checked back with her in the afternoon, and reassured us all that he didn't think anything was broken. That was a big relief.

When the train pulled into the Dearborn station in Chicago on the morning of the third day, we found a porter with a wheelchair waiting for us. Jim had asked the conductor to wire ahead and make the arrangements. A second porter collected all of our luggage, and then the two of them helped us to the shuttle bus that took us to Central Station. A few hours after arriving in Chicago, we were on board the Illinois Central and heading south.

I had my nose almost pressed to the window as I watched the landscape flow by outside. It was a beautiful late spring day. The recently seeded fields showed a haze of green along the ground, trees were sporting delicate new leaves, and everything seemed to be blossoming. After spending two years on the edge of the Sahara Desert, the lush fertility of central Illinois seemed almost artificial.

Finally, the next town was Rantoul. When the train stopped, we got up and began collecting our luggage with Jim once again taking charge. We got everything organized and as we got off the train we heard someone calling, "Bernice! Bernice, over here!" We looked around and saw Mr. Baier waving as he hurried toward us. After five days of travel and over seven thousand miles of adventure, we were home.

"It's impossible to say *'I can't'* without first saying *'I can.'*"

—Donna DeMuth

The King

... as told by Donna

We had recently returned to Paxton from Tripoli. Dad had to remain in Africa until the next February to fulfill his three-year assignment. So, it was Mom, Jim, Pat, Raymond and I sitting around the dinner table, sans Dad.

"Someone at this table has a special birthday coming up soon," Mom said teasingly.

I kind of rolled my eyes, but did not respond.

"What's so *special* about *her* birthday?" Pat asked.

"She's going to be sixteen," Mom brightly announced. "Would you like a sweet sixteen party, Sweetheart?"

"Oh, Mom, please. This is 1961, not 1861. No one has a sweet sixteen birthday party anymore."

"All right, but it should still be a special day. Is there a special gift you would like?"

"Not really ..."

Pat interrupted, "I still don't get it. What's so great about being sixteen?"

"I'll explain later, honey," Mom answered, cutting her short. Pat crossed her eyes at me when Mom looked away. *How childish* I thought. *Maybe she would grow up some day.* To put an end to her comments, I stuck my tongue out at her.

"I've got a good idea," Jim, my older brother said. "How would you like to catch the train to Chicago with me, and go and visit the Field museum. We could leave mid-morning, get to Chicago around noon, and have the entire afternoon to wander around the Natural History museum. What do you say? Would you like to do that?

"Just you and me?" I asked.

"Sure, why not?" It'll be my treat, I'll pay for everything, including your lunch."

I looked at him in surprise. Jim rarely volunteered to pay. Was he serious? I waited a minute or two, but he did not recant his offer, so I said, "Okay. I would like that a lot."

"That sounds like fun. It's a great idea for a special day!" Mom consented. "And I will pay for the train tickets as well."

"But what about us?" Patty cried.

"When Donna and Jim get back from Chicago, we'll still have a birthday party here at home. Then everyone will get to share the cake and ice cream, okay?"

"I guess so. But I want to go to Chicago, too,"

"When you have your sixteenth birthday, Patty, you can go to Chicago if you want to." My sister gave my mother a puzzled look, but seemed to be at a loss for words. I just smiled at her.

*   *   *

In 1961 my birthday fell on a Saturday, which made everything work out great. We had tickets to catch *The City of New Orleans* on its morning trip to Chicago. Jim said we would get into Grand Central Station right around 12:00 noon—perfect timing—and have a quick lunch before we went to the museum.

I was up early so that I had plenty of time to fix my hair and get dressed. Mom was hovering around me giving me motherly suggestions, and making me a little nervous. In fact, I believe she was more nervous than I could have ever been. I couldn't figure out why she was acting that way. It was another one of those mother-to-daughter mysteries.

She came into my room one last time to check what I was wearing.

"Oh dear, sweetheart, you're not wearing that, are you?" she sputtered.

"Yeah, I am. What's wrong with what I have on?" (I was wearing a new pair of blue jeans, folded up to my mid-calf, bobby socks and a new pair of saddle shoes. I topped this off with an over-sized man's white dress shirt with the sleeves rolled up to my elbows. All very hip.)

"Well, since it's your birthday, I thought you might like to dress up a little. One of your cotton summer dresses would be nice."

"Jim's wearing jeans, isn't he?"

"Yes, but he's a boy."

"So?" I asked looking her challengingly in the eyes.

"Tell you what," Mom gingerly advanced, "why don't you change your top for one of your pretty summer blouses. That will dress up your outfit like it was a special occasion. Agreed?"

"Okay." I put on a blue and white checkered sleeveless blouse. Mom was visibly relieved.

*   *   *

It was a beautiful day. The weather was perfect with a mild breeze and temperatures ranging in the mid- to high-seventies. The train was on time. Everything was going quite smoothly.

When we boarded the train, I saw Jim stop and talk to the conductor. I didn't wait, but went ahead and found our seats. As I was settling down by the window, the conductor walked directly towards me, with Jim following behind.

"Excuse me young lady," he said, stopping next to me. "I believe you are sitting in the wrong seat."

'No, I'm not. These are the seat numbers on our tickets. Show him, Jim."

"Now, don't argue with me, miss. Just quietly follow me and we will get this matter straightened out."

I questioningly looked at Jim. He just shrugged his shoulders. So, I got up and followed the conductor who was already headed down the aisle towards the front of the train. I had no idea what was going on, but I was concerned. Two more cars down, the conductor stopped, opened the door of the third car, and announced that our seats were 17A and 17B in that car. I stopped dead in my tracks. The third car was First Class!

He held the door open, and said, "I believe that, when a young lady turns sixteen, she should ride first class. Please enjoy your trip, miss." With that said, he formally led us to our seats.

I couldn't believe it. We were riding to Chicago sitting in these plush seats, and being waited on by stewards. Jim just sat there next to me grinning from ear to ear. I asked him if Mom had paid for these seats. He informed me that she had not, and it was the conductor's idea to "upgrade" our reservations. On top of that, I was served a small birthday cake with a candle on the top, and the steward sang *Happy Birthday* to me. Most of the passengers joined in. I did indeed feel special.

We arrived in Chicago fifteen minutes earlier than expected. Another good omen. Things were going better than planned. Jim suggested that we eat our lunch in the terminal. They had a pretty good diner in there, as well as a well-known restaurant. I opted to eat in the diner. I ordered a chicken salad sandwich with chips and a vanilla coke—in my world that was gourmet dining.

After lunch we looked in a couple of the gift shops, and then headed outside to go to the museum. Instead of walking in the direction of The Field Museum, Jim went down about half a block and stood by a taxi stand.

"What are you doing?" I asked. "The museum is just down there, about four blocks away. We can easily walk there from here."

"Since it's your birthday, I thought we'd take a taxi. Besides, there's some place I want to go before we hit the museum, and it's too far to walk"

"Okay … is it a secret or somethin'?

"Kind of—you'll see."

Before I could ask anything more, a taxi scooted across traffic and pulled up beside us at the curb. Jim stuck his head in the window and told the driver where he wanted to go. I couldn't make out what he had said with all the noise of the street blocking out his voice. He opened the back door for me, I climbed in, and we were off before Jim had enough time to completely close the door behind him.

This was totally unexpected. I didn't question Jim for more information. I just sat there looking out the window as we sped down the street. Finally we made this left turn onto another very wide, busy Chicago avenue. I could see small specialty restaurants, tourists' shops, and several theaters. There were people everywhere! Some were milling around the shops, others were lined up outside the restaurants, but the majority of them were in queues waiting outside the theaters. There was so much activity going on that I had not paid attention to what was playing at the theater our taxi pulled up to.

"This is our stop," Jim announced.

"Here? Why here?" I sputtered.

"Don't ask. Just get out of the taxi. You'll know soon enough."

Jim helped me out and ushered me through the crowd of people right into the theater. "We don't have to stand in line. I already have our tickets," he shouted at me over all the noise.

We stepped aside of the milling crowd to get our bearing, and I finally had a chance to see where we were. In fact, almost in front of me standing by a rack of playbills, was this huge cardboard cutout of Elvis Presley. I gasped and grabbed Jim's arm just above his elbow.

"Are we …? I mean … Do we have tickets to see Elvis?

"Happy sixteenth birthday, Donna."

I couldn't get my breath. I stood there with my mouth hanging open. My legs felt shaky and everything in the theater lobby appeared over-bright. I needed to sit down before I passed out.

Jim leaned over and said in my ear," "Take some slow, deep breaths," as he led me to a bench along the wall.

"I don't believe it. I've got to be dreaming. Are we really going to see Elvis? What about the museum?"

"Yes, if you can get yourself together, we are going to see Elvis. We have seats in the first row of the second balcony. It was the best I could do. But, if you would rather go to the museum instead …"

"No, I don't want to go to the museum, and I don't care where we sit as long as we get to go in there," I said as I pointed to one of the open theater doors.

"Then that's precisely where we are going. You just let me know when you're ready."

*　　　　　*　　　　　*

How can I describe the thrill of being in that theater that day? It wasn't even on my dream list—I never thought it could happen.

We found our seats with the help of an usher. We were in the first row in the second balcony just like Jim said. There were no obstructions in front of us to prevent a clear and total view of the stage. The performers would be small and hard to see, but I didn't care. After we got settled, Jim pointed out the binocular holders on the balcony rail directly in front of each seat. To unlock the holder, you had to insert one dollar of change in the coin slot on the top. I thought that was too much to pay to rent binoculars. Jim responded with "the sky's the limit" bravado, and rented a pair for us to share.

There was a lead band that opened the show. I don't remember their name. When Elvis was introduced, the screaming and hysteria began. I loved it! All that pandemonium was part of the *Elvis thing*.

The binoculars worked quite well. I could see the sweat running down his face, those beautiful thick black eyelashes, and that crooked grin of his. He sang all of my favorite songs, and the funny thing about that was, in spite of the noise, I could clearly make out every word he sang. I didn't scream or yell—I was too shy to do that. But I did have goose bumps all over me. I sat on the very edge of my chair, hanging onto the balcony rail throughout the entire concert. Many years later I took my twelve-year-old daughter to see Elvis in concert in Ft. Worth, Texas. She did the very same things.

The concert ended after many encores. Jim and I waited until the stage was completely dark, the stage lights shut off, and most of the fans had left. I remember slowly exiting the theater, and standing by the taxi stand trying to get a cab to the train station. I vaguely recall thanking Jim for the best birthday gift I had ever received. I don't remember saying a whole lot more.

After we got seated in the train, I asked Jim if it was all right if I didn't talk a lot. He nodded his head and said "sure," grinning the whole time.

I don't know what happened, but when the train reached Kankakee the dam burst forth. I started chattering non-stop, barely taking a breath between exclamations. I bombarded Jim with all my feelings about the concert: the perspiration, the eyelashes, the crooked smile, my favorite songs, etc., etc.

Finally I stopped, paused, and asked him, "Did I thank you already?"

"Only three times," he answered.

"Oh. Jim, what makes Elvis so special?"

"Elvis is one of a kind, and he belongs to our generation. He treats his music as an individual and appears not to be willing to betray himself. He stands alone, and takes all the guff quietly and shyly. He's a leader to all us *World War II babies*. History will prove that our generation was very unique, and rock 'n' roll was a big sign of our time. Believe me, it's here to stay!"

*   *   *

When we got off the train in Paxton, Mom was waiting for us with Patty and Raymond in tow. I ran up to her and gave her a big long hug.

"Oh, Mom, you were right. This has been the best birthday, ever! I can't thank you and Jim enough."

"The look on your face is all the thanks I need, Sweetheart."

"What's the big deal?" Patty asked. "You just went to the museum. Why are there tears in your eyes, Donna?"

"We didn't go to the museum, at all. Jim took me to see Elvis Presley in concert instead!"

"What? You're foolin' me, aren't you?" Patty croaked.

"Nope, and I have the playbill to prove it." (That quickly shut her up. That is until we got home, and she nagged me for every detail of every minute we were at the concert.)

*   *   *

Mom said we would have my birthday celebration at home the next day. She figured I had enough excitement for one day. I was tired that night when I went to bed; blissfully tired, but I couldn't sleep. So I went downstairs to talk to Mom (just she and I).

"Does Dad know I went to see *Elvis the Pelvis*, as he would say?" I asked.

"Yes, he does," Mom replied. "He said he couldn't understand it all, but if that was what you wanted, it was okay with him. In his book it was just a lot of hog swaller."

"*Of course*," I smiled to myself. He would have the last word and get his two cents worth spoken.

"I must admit, Mom, that I was a little surprised that you approved."

"Believe it or not, Sweetheart, I was sixteen myself once. Back then it was the *Big Band Days*, and we had Glenn Miller and Tommy Dorsey to get excited about. My generation had this *thing* about Frank Sinatra, and I would challenge your generation to a match of screaming, squealing and fainting any day.

"No kidding."

"No kidding, Sweetheart, and your grandparents thought we were silly to spend our hard-earned money to go and hear them play, when we could just as well have listened to the radio. I do understand that all teenagers from any generation must have their own time and space. It's all part of growing up and making your unique mark on the world."

"You know what, Mom, you're pretty cool as far as mothers go, and I'm very lucky to be your daughter. I'll swap you an Elvis record for a Frank Sinatra platter."

"If you have no regrets, you need to get out more."

—Anonymous

Matchmaker, Matchmaker

… as told by Donna

"Who was on the phone?" asked my mother as I walked into the kitchen.

"It was for me. Eddie Morton called and asked me out." I paused, thinking. "How strange. I hardly know him."

Mom turned and looked at me with an unspoken questioning look.

"I see him at school all the time. He's a year ahead of me, and he's in the Catholic teen club …" I said to myself more than to my Mother, "But why would he call me?"

"His mother is in the Catholic Women's Club with me, and I've gotten to know her," Mom said. "She's a very nice person, and I'm sure Eddie is too."

I stopped in my tracks! I think I had just received the answer to my puzzlement about Eddie.

"Mom, you didn't have anything to do with that phone call, did you?"

"Well, Edith and I were talking the other day, and the subject of our teenagers somehow came up in the conversation. I told her how proud I was of you—that you gave me little trouble, what a good student you were, and how you are a very helpful daughter. She had just as many nice things to say about Eddie. He is a good Catholic boy, you know."

"Mom, for crying-out-loud! Don't arrange dates for me!"

"I didn't arrange a date for you!" Mom said defensively. "I merely made the comment that it would be nice if you got to be friends with Eddie, and Edith agreed."

"Oh, I'm sure she did! Nobody goes out with Eddie Morton! I can't believe I said 'yes.'"

"You did! You said yes!" Mom composed herself and put a lid on her enthusiasm. "I'm sure you will have a good time. Where is he taking you?"

"He asked me to go and play tennis with him this coming Saturday."

"Tennis! But, you don't know how to play tennis!"

"I know. But Dad does. I thought I'd ask him to explain the game to me and give me a few pointers."

"I don't think it's that simple, Sweetheart."

I could tell that Mom was concerned. "Don't worry. It's only Eddie Morton. I'll just fake it."

"Maybe your father could give you a few lessons before Saturday. Why don't you ask him?"

"Okay, I will. But, like I said, it's no big deal."

Trying to interject some hope into the conversation, Mom asked what I would wear to my tennis game. I replied, "Shorts and a blouse, I suppose. I doubt Eddie will notice."

"Oh, dear," she sighed.

*   *   *

That evening I asked Dad about the tennis lessons. I did not expect his reaction. He flat out refused! He added that there was "no way in this blue heaven" that he could teach me to play tennis in one or two lessons! I persisted, though. In other words, I nagged him until he agreed. Finally, he consented to show me how to play tennis starting Wednesday evening after supper.

It was a disaster! I learned that it was impossible to become a tennis star after a couple lessons. Dad went easy on me, but I missed every return. I also quickly learned that it is very, very hard to chase after that little ball around the court and not mess up your hair. On the last serve from Dad, I thought I might, just might, be able to return the ball. I was backing up and backing up trying to determine where the ball was going to come down, when I stepped on the end of the court's concrete, twisted my ankle, and landed on my butt in the grass. Dad ran to my aid and helped me to my feet. "Can you stand on it?" he asked me. I could, but it really hurt. When I tried to walk, I couldn't help limping. Dad assisted me home to have Mother put an ace bandage of my ankle, and declared that there was no way I was going to play tennis on *that* ankle on Saturday. It seemed God helps those who can't help themselves!

I called Eddie and told him about my sports injury, hoping to squeeze out of the date. No such luck. He graciously said it was no problem, and we could go to a movie instead. *West Side Story* was playing in Champaign, and he wanted to see it. He would pick me up at seven o'clock on Saturday. Oh well, there was just so much one can ask from God. I was on my own.

*   *   *

The movie was crowded, and we had to stand in line for a while. It was worth it. I also wanted to see *West Side Story*, and was excited about being there. As we inched our way forward in line, Eddie took the opportunity to inform me about: how the movie was the re-telling of *Romeo and Juliet* set in present time (*like I didn't know*), that it was his policy not to buy food or beverages at a movie theater because they charged three times what they were worth (*cheapskate*), and about a small step that was located at the beginning of the theater aisle that one could easily trip over (*Okay, okay, I'll watch for it*).

As I said, the theater was crowded, and there was a line going into the movie, as well as the line we had stood in to get our tickets. There was some gentle pushing and shoving—people were eager to get to their seats before the film started. Just as we reached the aisle threshold, Eddie held up his hand like a traffic cop, stopped the forward movement of the rest of the line behind us, and loudly pointed out the small step he had warned me about earlier.

"Now, remember this step when we leave the theater, Donna. You could trip on it and fall down! Then I would have to sue the theater. Ha, ha!"

Voices behind us muttered, "Just keep moving. What's the hold up. Did someone trip?"

Oh, my God, I was so embarrassed I could have died! *What had I gotten myself into by agreeing to this date! Once we get in our seats, maybe the movie will keep him quiet!* I literally grabbed Eddie's arm and jerked him forward.

We found two seats together just past the mid-center of the theater, right next to another young couple. The seats weren't on the aisle, but they were well positioned for watching the movie, which started minutes after we got settled down.

West Side Story has got to be one of the best musicals made for the screen. From the very beginning, it holds your attention until the last note at the end. I was actually excited to be sitting in that theater, and could not imagine any way Eddie could screw this up for me.

He was on his best behavior, until Richard Beymer began to sing *Maria*. Eddie burst out in song and sang along with the star word by word! He was even gesturing with his arms as though he was performing to the audience! I was stunned! The people sitting around us were shushing him or bluntly telling him to "be quiet." He ignored them and continued to sing, "*I just met a girl named Maria.*" I wanted to disappear right there and then. There was no place I could escape to! The only action I could take was to lean closer and closer to the young man sitting next to me on my other side, hoping people would think that *he* was my date. He scrunched closer to his date. I was invading his territory. The three of us were all slanted away from Eddie.

Eddie did not stop his accompaniment throughout the entire movie. I am surprised he wasn't thrown out of the theater.

When the movie ended, I quickly moved to the end of our row and merged with the people in the aisle. I managed to get a couple of people between Eddie and myself. I couldn't help hearing him, when he entered the aisle, call out. "Donna, Donna, wait up! And watch out for that step!" I acted as though I didn't know who he was. I was on a mission—to get out of there before anyone realized that I was with him!

Just then I heard a loud thump behind me and a woman's voice exclaim, "Oh, my goodness, someone help him!"

My whole world went into slow motion. I turned my head carefully, and, with perfect clarity, saw a small group of people stopped at the end of the aisle (where that small step was located), staring down at Eddie who had managed to trip over the step and was lying face down on the floor. The next five minutes are all a blur to me; I don't remember how we got out of the theater and into the car.

As calmly as I could, I explained to Eddie, "No, I don't feel like stopping and having coffee. My ankle is really hurting me, and I think I need to go directly home and soak my foot in Epsom salts" (something I would have loved to do to his head). He expressed his sympathy, put the car in gear, and, to my immense relief, started towards Paxton.

We were approximately thirty miles from my house. It was the longest ride of my life! He made me sit next to him in the car, and somehow had managed to slip his arm around my shoulders. He seemed to be driving as slow as he could. Every time we hit a red light, he would bend towards me, jerk me around and plant a kiss as close as he could to my mouth, sometimes hitting the target. He was a "bug smasher!" By that, I mean that he would kiss you with his lips tightly clamped together, connect to your face or lips with force, and then press his lips against you as though he was trying to smash a bug on a window pane. After one or two kisses, it began to hurt. All the way home, I'm certain Eddie was thinking "come on light; turn red." I, on the other hand, was thinking; "come on light, turn green."

Finally we hit the open highway between Champaign and Paxton. At least there were no traffic lights to contend with. I turned the radio on in his car as a deterrent to conversation. I just wanted to sit quietly and get home as fast as we could.

An Elvis song came on the radio. I have been an Elvis fan from day one, and I was moving with the rhythm of the song (not one of my favorites, but a song with a catchy beat). All of a sudden Eddie burst into song again, "*I just wanna be your Eddie bear.*"

He was messing with an Elvis song; this was the last straw! I could not help myself. I exclaimed, "For God sakes will you knock it off! Who told you that you could sing!?"

"My mother thinks I could be a professional," he said in a small voice.

"A professional what!?"

He didn't answer me, and we rode the rest of the way home in complete silence.

*   *   *

I dashed from his car and into our house faster than he could say good-night. Mom and Dad were still up, because I was home a lot earlier than normal. I slammed the door shut behind me and stomped into the living room. Mom had a surprised look on her face.

"You're home early, sweetheart. How was your date?" she asked.

"Don't say a word to me! In fact, don't speak to me for the rest of my life! Good night!

As I stomped up the stairs, I could hear muffled giggling coming from the bedroom I shared with my little sister. *Since I couldn't kill Eddie, she seemed to be a good candidate for second choice!*

*   *   *

Mom didn't pressure me for an explanation of my bad mood until the following evening. I was in such a funk that neither Mom nor Dad said a word while I ranted and raved about my date with Eddie. When I was done, I must admit I felt better after getting it all off my chest. After a brief pause, Dad said, "Eddie sounds like a looney to me." And then he went back to reading his newspaper.

"I'm sorry your date went so badly, Sweetheart," Mom sympathized. "I'm afraid he may call back to make another date. What will you do?"

"I don't know yet, but I will let him down easy (*unless he pushes me*). I am not going out with him again, ever!"

Mom was right; he did call back, not once, but several times. Let's see … the first time I had a summer cold, the second time I had a toothache, next I had to baby-sit my little brother, and then I had a migraine, etc., etc.

The last time I was on the phone with him Mom had walked through the room and overheard me talking to Eddie. After I hung up she said, "You can go to hell for lying as well as stealing, Donna."

"HE wouldn't dare! I am the only girl who actually went out on a date with Eddie Morton! That's enough punishment for an eternity."

"Having an older sister is like having a compass to guide you through life."

—Lucy, *Peanuts*

I Think We're Alone, Now

... as told by Pat

"Pat, why don't you come out to the kitchen with me? I could use some help with dinner tonight."

I looked up at my mom and said, "What? You want *me* to help *cook?*" Cooking had never been one of my strong points.

"Yes, I want you to help me. I'm fixing a pot roast, and you can help peel the potatoes and clean the carrots. Let's go."

"Okay, no problem." I set aside the magazine that I had been thumbing through and trailed after Mom into the kitchen. While she started pulling out pots and pans, I got the bag of potatoes and dumped a bunch of them into the sink. After collecting a paring knife from the drawer, I started peeling.

Mom fussed with the roast for a few minutes, and soon had it searing in the big roaster on top of the stove. While she waited for the first side to brown she casually asked me, "So, how are things going for you at school this year?"

"Oh, okay. It's just school."

"Well, it is your second year in high school. I thought perhaps your classes were getting a little more interesting for you."

"Naw—my schedule is still mostly required classes and I don't get to pick electives until next year. Other than that it's just school."

Mom turned the roast over, and continued, "Are you getting to know more of your classmates and all?"

"Mom, I've known my classmates since first grade."

"Well, of course you have. But now you're having classes with other kids than just them, aren't you?"

"Yeah, I guess. And I'm getting to know some of the kids in Thespians Club."

"Well, that's good." She added some salt and pepper to the roast, covered it tightly, and turned down the flame. "Do you know Dwight Smith?"

"Who?"

"Dwight Smith. I think he might be a year or two ahead of you."

I thought for a few seconds, and then placed a face with the name. "Oh, you mean DeWayne Smith. Yeah, well, I know who he is, but I don't know him like a friend.

"I thought his name was Dwight?"

"Yeah, well, his full name is Dwight DeWayne Smith, but he uses his middle name. He's always correcting people about how to pronounce it. He insists on what he calls the "French" pronunciation, you know, like *DuhWayne*, so a lot of the kids call him Doo-Wayne."

"Is his family French?"

"I don't know. I think he just likes to be different. He took French his first two years in school, and now he runs around trying to be continental. Why?"

"Oh, I met his mother the other day. We're both on the refreshment committee for the PTA Spring Fair, and we got to visiting a little after the meeting."

"I've never met his parents."

"She seemed like a very nice lady. She told me that Dwight is a very good student."

"He's on the Honor Roll a lot, and I think he belongs to The National Honor Society."

"You can always tell. Good kids come from good families. You know, while we were talking it seemed to us that you and Dwight have a lot in common. You both read a lot, and you're both excellent students." There was a weighted pause before she added, "You might think about getting to know him a little better."

I looked over my shoulder at Mom, but she was concentrating on the stove and her roast again. Discussing eligible young men with my mother had always given me a funny feeling, but I decided to gloss over it. My reply was a neutral, "Yeah, I might do that. Are these enough potatoes?"

"Yes, Dear, that's fine. Now, if you'll just clean that bunch of carrots for me, that'll be a big help."

*   *   *

It was strange, but after that conversation with Mom it seemed that DeWayne Smith kept popping up in my near vicinity at school. Between classes he strolled past my locker, I kept bumping into him in the halls, and at lunch he always seemed to be seated at the next table in the cafeteria. He did stand out from the crowd—it was early 1964 and more casual dress was inching its way into the halls of Paxton High. We were teetering on the brink of the hippie movement, and the Beatles and the Rolling Stones were taking over America. Amid the sea of jeans, tee-shirts, and longer hair, DeWayne stood out like a sore thumb; a monument to conservatism wearing his dress slacks, neatly pressed sport shirts, highly polished shoes, and closely trimmed crew cut hair.

On a warm afternoon in April I came out of school and started walking home. I hadn't gone a hundred feet down Center Street before DeWayne was beside me. Very casually, he cleared his throat and said, "Hi! It looks like we're going the same way. Do you mind if I walk with you?"

I glanced over at him and replied, "Oh, sure."

"Um-m-m-m, I don't think we've actually met, have we? I'm DeWayne Smith, and you're Pat DeMuth, aren't you? I was in French class with your sister last year; maybe she mentioned me?"

"Nice to meet you, DeWayne."

"Enchanté."

I looked over at him, and then said, "Yeah, I think Donna did say something about you in French class." I didn't tell him that Donna had said he was an insufferable teacher's pet and show-off.

"Yes, I thought she would have. She seemed to be a very pleasant person. By the way, is your family French? I would assume so from the way your last name is spelled."

An image of my boisterous German/Belgian grandfather hit my mind. I grinned and replied, "I don't think so, unless the French are into oompah polka bands, beer, and sauerkraut."

"Oh! Well, that's a surprise."

"The name was originally German and spelled with a small 'm' in it. There's a long, tangled history that includes a burgher-meister or two, religious persecution, and whatnot. Our branch of the family finally gave up on Europe as hopeless and emigrated. Of course, my dad says that any family

worth it's salt has at least a couple of horse-thieves and con-men hanging from
the family tree."

DeWayne looked shocked, so I thought it prudent to add, "It's a joke,
DeWayne."

"Oh! I see. Yes, of course. Heh, heh, heh."

We had now reached Washington Street, and I said, "Well, DeWayne, it
was nice talking to you, but I turn here."

"I thought you were going home?"

"I am, and I need to turn here to get there."

"I thought you lived on High Street, over by the park."

"Well, I do live on High Street, just not that part of it. A lot of people don't
know that there's a break in the street at the elementary school and Memorial
Field. Over on the other side of Memorial Field it picks up again off Summer
Street and goes on for another block. That's where I live."

"I didn't know that. Well, heh, heh, heh, if I wanted to take you home I
guess I'd need a car, wouldn't I?"

"Pretty much so." I decided to be polite and not point out that I walked
between home and school several times a week.

"Well, heh, heh, that gives me an idea. There's a good movie showing
down on campus this weekend. Would you like to go with me on Friday or
Saturday night?"

"Oh, gosh, thanks, but I'm afraid I can't. My parents won't let me date
until I'm sixteen."

"Really? When's your birthday?"

"Not until September. I can go to stuff like school events and dances, as
long as I'm home on time, but not a real date yet."

"Oh, that's too bad. I'm sure you would like the movie. Well …" DeWayne
shuffled around a little bit, and seemed to be at a sudden loss for words.

My armful of books was getting heavy, so I said, "Yeah. Well, look, I gotta
go. I'll see you around school."

"Okay."

I turned to the right and started south on Washington Street. After a few
moments, I glanced back over my shoulder and saw that DeWayne had continued east on Center Street.

Over the next few weeks, DeWayne continued to pop up all over the
school. He made a point of saying "Hi," to me when he saw me in the halls,
and if time allowed (like at lunch hour) he would stop me and chat a bit. I had
already formed the opinion that DeWayne was a bit of a dork, to use the

phraseology of the time. He was always nice to me but he could bore the legs off a table, and I had yet to discover even a glimmer of a sense of humor in him. Getting to know him better and going out on a date with him were not items on my priority list.

Then, on a Tuesday in mid May, DeWayne dangled the ultimate bait in front of me—he asked me to go to a Peter, Paul and Mary concert with him at the University of Illinois. Peter, Paul and Mary! These were popular artists and you heard their songs on the radio—the *real* radio—WLS out of Chicago! This was a chance to see them in person, to be in the same building with them, and to hear them singing their songs for real. I was dazzled by the possibility.

Reality struck back. The vision dissolved into mist as Dad's voice echoed in my head saying, "No dating until you're sixteen, and home no later than ten o'clock if you're going to a school dance." I reminded DeWayne of my restrictions. He just smiled and asked me if I would go with him *if* my parents would agree. With the magic of the concert clouding my reason once more, I told him I would go, but I didn't have the first idea of how to get Dad to agree to it. DeWayne told me to leave it up to him. I agreed, but really didn't think he had much chance of success.

In that regard, I totally underestimated DeWayne. He called my dad and set up a time when he could meet with my parents. I knew nothing about this until DeWayne showed up at our door on Friday evening, starched, pressed, brushed and polished as usual. His manners were impeccable—he shook hands with Dad and called him "sir." When Mom entered the room carrying a tray of coffee and cookies, DeWayne sprang to his feet as if he had been launched out of his chair. He swept the tray out of her hands and carefully placed it in the center of the coffee table, remaining on his feet until after she was seated. He complimented her on her charming home, and then spent a few minutes discussing current events with both of them.

Knowing my family as I did, I figured something would happen to disturb this cozy social scene, and I was absolutely right. My seven-year-old brother, Raymond, marched into the room, grabbed a handful of cookies, and positioned himself directly in front of DeWayne. Ray looked him over, and then demanded, "Who are *you*, and what are you doing here?"

"Well, I'm DeWayne Smith, but I don't think I know who you are?"

Dad provided the identifying information. "This is our youngest son, Raymond."

DeWayne stuck out his hand and said, "Well, I'm very pleased to meet you, Master DeMuth."

Ray's eyes widened a bit, he ignored the hand, and blew a very wet raspberry (with a liberal amount of cookie crumbs) right at DeWayne. He then stuck *his* hand out, palm up, and said, "Give me a quarter and I'll go away."

DeWayne reeled back a bit, and Mom quickly admonished my brother.

"Raymond Douglas, you are being rude to our guest. Now, apologize and then go to your room."

Ray looked DeWayne up and down again, grabbed another handful of cookies, and then turned and stomped out of the room. Mom smoothed over the situation with a murmured apology and, after a few moments of awkward silence, the conversation picked up again.

DeWayne was a member of the debate team at school, and it was a well-earned position. He deftly eased the conversation to the issue of the concert, and began presenting his arguments in a logical progression. By the time he left, about an hour later, Mom and Dad had agreed that I could go to the concert with him, as well as allowing him to take me to dinner beforehand. DeWayne assured them that he wouldn't take me anywhere near any of the questionable bars around campus where alcohol was served without proper ID, and he would have me home shortly after the concert, which meant sometime around midnight. He also obtained their blessings on taking me to some movies over the summer. After he left, Mom and Dad spent a little time talking about what a fine young man he was. I couldn't believe it.

*   *   *

I spent the next two weeks in a frenzy of anticipation. During this time, Donna came home from college to spend the summer. I immediately told her about the concert. She had seen Peter, Paul and Mary in concert in Seattle and told me all about it and how great it had been, immediately notching my excitement up even higher. We then put our heads together and began planning all the details of my outfit for this big event.

We decided that I should wear one of my new sundresses that had skinny little spaghetti straps, the current fashion rage among the high school set. Since a regular bra would never work with that type of dress, I had to wear a strapless corset under it, something my mother called a "merry widow." It's rather like wearing a very tight, full-body cast—bending or turning at the waist becomes an impossibility, and even something as simple as breathing has to be carefully planned. I quickly decided that corsets were a legacy from the Spanish Inquisition.

DeWayne picked me up at six in the evening, and the first thing on the itinerary was dinner at a fancy restaurant in Champaign. When the waiter came to our table, DeWayne ordered for both of us, which grated on my nerves a little bit. (For heaven's sake, I was certainly capable of figuring out for myself what I liked to eat!) Of course, he first ordered in French, but that only earned him a blank stare from the waiter. With a condescending sigh, DeWayne repeated the order in English: we would be having lobster tails, baked potatoes, and tossed salad with (what else?) French dressing. He then ordered ice water to go with the meal, and *café au lait* for afterwards.

I had been thinking about the roast beef and mashed potatoes, with a Coke on the side. I had never had lobster before in my life and had no idea whether I would even like it, but it appeared that I was going to have it. Our meal arrived, and after the first, tiny taste of the lobster I decided to forgive DeWayne—lobster was delicious! I had two more bites of lobster, a bite of salad, and a bite of the baked potato. As I lifted my fourth bite of lobster on my fork, I realized that I was feeling rather strange. The piece of lobster suddenly appeared to be huge, and my stomach was frantically trying to send a message to my brain—*don't even try it!* The merry widow had struck! With my torso savagely clamped in this modern Iron Maiden, there simply wasn't enough room left to consider consuming a meal. I spent the rest of dinner pushing the food around on my plate, pretending to eat, and finally watched in misery as the waiter carried three quarters of that lovely lobster back to the kitchen.

After dinner, it was on to the concert. The Assembly Hall was sold out and packed to the rafters with excited people. Peter, Paul and Mary came onstage to a roar of approval, and the next three hours were magical. I was immersed in the music, the personalities of the performers, and the entire atmosphere of the concert. The only thing that marred the evening was that I found myself getting more and more uncomfortable as time passed. Besides the merry widow (which seemed to get tighter the longer one wore it), no one had warned me what six hours in heels can do to feet. I became as anxious about midnight as Cinderella, and would have been delighted to leave my high heels on the steps of the building as I rushed for home.

The drive home from Champaign passed in a haze. I was going over the concert in my mind, humming snatches of the songs, and reliving each magical moment to imprint it firmly in my memory. I have no idea if DeWayne talked to me or if I answered him all the way home. When he pulled into our driveway, I was amazed that we had arrived there so quickly. For a goodnight kiss, DeWayne leaned over and pecked me on my cheek, then made sure I was safely inside the house before he left.

The moment I was inside the door, I pried my shoes off and hobbled up to my room. Off came the sundress, and then I set about unhooking the thousand or so hooks down the front of the corset. As the last hook released, I gasped in a huge breath of air. The next instant, I realized I was ravenous. I quickly pulled on some shorts and a comfortable top, and then crammed my swollen feet into my slippers.

I ran back downstairs and hit the kitchen like a famine victim, yanking open the refrigerator door and grabbing for anything edible. After some olives, a couple of pickles, and a carrot I slowed down enough to put together a quick bologna sandwich. I carried the sandwich upstairs to my room and ate it while I sat at my desk. Each bite was spiced with another pang of regret for that lobster.

*　　　*　　　*

Suddenly, summer was upon us and, along with the warm weather, I discovered that I had a problem to deal with. That problem was Doo-Wayne Smith. He began calling two or three times a week, asking me to go play tennis, to accompany him to an art show at the University, or to go to a movie. On some of the calls, he just wanted to "talk" which meant I was stuck on the phone for up to an hour listening while he informed me of his opinions on a multitude of subjects.

Now, remember, this was 1964 and attitudes about phones were different than today. Paxton still didn't even have a dial system in place. In our house there was only one phone, it was located on the end table by the couch in the living room, and it was hard-wired into the wall. Any conversation on it was conducted in the presence of anyone else in the living room at the time. My parents also frequently pointed out that they paid for a phone for the convenience of the entire family, and it was very rude for anyone to monopolize it for idle chit-chat. When Doo-Wayne went into one of his monologues, I would try to cut it short by saying I had chores to do, but my protests fell on deaf ears. He would just rattle on and, as the time dragged on, I would be on the receiving end of withering glares from my father.

A couple of times I tried telling him that I simply had to go and hung up. He would wait ten minutes, call back, and pick up again right where he had left off. Once I tried just hanging up with no warning. Moments later the phone rang again, and it was DeWayne complaining that the phone system had cut him off.

I couldn't figure out how he came up with enough things to talk about for so long until one phone call when he stopped suddenly and asked me to wait for a moment. I could hear some faint shuffling noises in the background. When I asked him what happened, he told me he had dropped his cards. He then told me that he made notes about interesting things he came across, and used those note cards so he wouldn't forget anything. I couldn't believe it—this jerk used *cue cards* for his phone calls!

One Saturday morning Donna and I planned to go shopping in Champaign. We promised Mom that we would get the cleaning done before we left, and we were industriously dusting, vacuuming, and scrubbing when the phone rang. It was Doo-Wayne, and he wanted to talk. I stammered around a little bit trying to get him off the phone, but it didn't work.

The next thing I knew, Donna snatched the receiver from my hand and placed it on the cushion of the couch. She dragged me away from the phone and whispered intently to me, "Look, we'll never get this done if you sit on the phone for an hour. Let's keep cleaning, and whenever one of us gets near the phone we'll pick up the receiver and murmur something encouraging. All he wants anyway is an audience."

We put the plan into action, and at first Doo-Wayne wasn't even aware of my absence. We finished with the living room and moved into the dining room, which resulted in longer delays before one of us would remember to go snatch up the phone and say something inconsequential. Then we were in the kitchen, rubbing and scrubbing as fast as we could so that we could soon be on our way to doing something fun.

We were almost finished when Mom walked into the kitchen and calmly said, "Girls, the couch seems to be trying to talk to someone. Would either of you know anything about that?"

Donna and I looked at each other in horror—we had completely forgotten about Doo-Wayne! I raced into the living room to grab the phone, but the receiver had disappeared. It had slipped down between the arm of the couch and the cushion. A muffled voice was coming from under the cushion asking, "Pat? Pat? Are you there?" I grabbed the cord to the receiver and started reeling it in. It got stuck, so I yanked. Finally, I had it in my hand and clamped it to my ear as I said, "Sorry, DeWayne, my mom said something to me and I got distracted."

"Oh, I see. Well, as I was saying ..."

I abruptly cut across him. "Look, DeWayne, Mom wants me to go somewhere with her right now. I gotta go. Bye." I hung up the phone and looked up. Donna was sitting limply in a dining room chair, laughing her head off, while Mom stood in the doorway of the living room giving me one of her "Mother Looks." Mom looked from one of us to the other, then just shook her head and went off to her sewing room without a word.

All of this had further convinced me that Doo-Wayne was a pretentious bore, and I really didn't want to encourage him any further. I kept coming up with excuses for not going out (a baby-sitting job was always a good one), but he was a determined young man who did not give up easily. The assault on my resistance continued and intensified, and I didn't know how to stop it. I finally decided that I needed some advice from my sister.

*   *   *

I chose a quiet evening when Donna was in her room. I tapped on her doorframe as I poked my head into her room and asked, "Hey, are you busy?"

"No, not really. What's up?"

"I've got a problem I need to talk to you about, if you've got the time."

"Oh, sure. Come on in. What's the problem?"

She was sitting at her desk, so I walked in and settled down on the side of her bed before I answered. "In two words: Doo-Wayne Smith."

"Right. He *has* turned into a pain in the butt, hasn't he?"

"Yeah, and I don't know what to do about it."

"Why in the world did you ever go out with him in the first place?"

"Well ... It was Peter, Paul and Mary, you know?"

"Sure I know. So, did you have fun at the concert?"

"The concert was great, but not because of Doo-Wayne."

"Have you tried telling him to take a long walk on a short pier?"

"I was going to, but then Mom talked to me about him the other day."

"And what did she say?"

"She said I should have known what he was like before I went out with him, and that if I only went out with him to get to the concert, I wasn't being fair. She said that was using him. That if I agreed to go out with him, it was natural that he thought I liked him, and he spent a lot of money trying to show me a good time. She also pointed out that the concert wasn't the usual dating situation and didn't give us much time to talk or get to know each other better. She thinks that maybe if I went out with him to something more relaxed, like a movie, I might actually get to like him. She thinks I should give him a second chance. She really made me feel like a crumb."

"Yeah, well, she's good at that. It's part of being a mom."

"But that doesn't change the fact that Doo-Wayne is still a jerk."

"No, but Mom does have a point about the concert. Maybe you should go to a movie with him, or even two, and then you can tell him that you want to break it off. At least that's more private than trying to tell him over the phone."

I groaned. "But that means spending another evening with Doo-Wayne."

"Yeah, but at least then everyone will be satisfied that you gave him a fair chance." Donna paused for a second, and then asked, "Listen, he isn't a masher, is he?"

"A what?"

"A masher. You know, after the concert did he try to jump your bones, or want to go out in the country and neck?"

"Oh. No, in fact, I got a peck on the cheek as a goodnight kiss. At first I thought he was just going to shake my hand or something."

"Well, that's good. Although, you know, if you do go out with him again he may think that you actually like him. He may want to do some necking. I don't think you've done any of that yet, so you need to be prepared."

"What do you mean?"

Donna turned in her chair and focused her entire attention on me. I immediately recognized the signs that I was about to get some really juicy older sister advice, and I leaned forward eagerly. She collected her thoughts and began, "Well, first of all, you need to know that different guys kiss differently, and in high school most of them don't know how to do it all that well. I've kind of categorized them. First of all, there's The Grouper."

"The what?"

"The Grouper. You've seen pictures of those big tropical fish with the big rubbery lips that always seem to be gulping?"

A vivid image filled my mind as I nodded in answer.

"Well, that's how a Grouper comes at you—all rubbery lips and mouth. And when he makes contact, it feels like he's trying to suck your face off. The best thing you can do with a Grouper is try to avoid it, or carry a bunch of

Kleenex with you in case you can't. At least you can use the tissue to dry your face."

"How do you avoid it?"

"We'll get to that. Second, there's The Bug Smasher. Now, this guy acts like you've got a bug sitting on your lips, and it's his job to kill that bug using only his lips. He'll get his lips all scrunched and pinched up hard, and then grind down on yours. Spend too much time with a Bug Smasher, and you'll have a fat lip the next day. A little bottle of Numzit helps."

"Yuck! Are they *all* that bad?"

"Wait a minute, there's another one you need to watch out for, and that's The Bullfrog. Um-m-m-m, do you know what a French kiss is?"

"Yeah, I think so. Isn't that where a guy puts his tongue in your mouth?"

"Right, but The Bullfrog has watched way too many bad movies. This guy has the longest, fastest tongue in the world, and he acts like a frog that just spotted a big, juicy fly sitting on your tonsils. The best advice I can give you there is to keep your mouth shut and your lips together, no matter what."

"Okay, so back to my question. How do you avoid all this?"

"As he's moving in to plant The Big One on you, you can pretend to spot something over his shoulder. You move your head to the side and say something like, 'Oh, isn't that a barn owl?' He'll usually end up hitting your cheek or ear, because he won't be ready for that little head move. Another thing, particularly if they want to neck out in the driveway when they bring you home, is to tell them that Dad waits up for us. Tell him that if you're not in the house within five minutes, Dad will come out to get you—that normally cools any passion."

"Well, for Heaven's sake. Why does anyone even *want* to neck with a guy?"

"Every now and again, you'll find someone who knows what he's doing, and then it's pretty nice. You know what the old saying is, don't you? When you're trying to find your Prince Charming, you have to kiss a lot of toads along the way."

Donna grinned at me as I was suddenly hit with a fit of the giggles. Within seconds, we were both laughing like loons. We were sisters, confidantes and, most of all, best friends. I had really missed my sister while she had been away at college.

*   *   *

Taking Donna's advice, I agreed to go to a movie with Doo-Wayne, and then, a few weeks later, a second one. Both evenings were exactly the same. Instead of going to a popular movie, Doo-Wayne insisted on going to foreign "art films" showing on campus at the University of Illinois in Urbana. The movies were the kind where an actor chatters in a foreign language for about two minutes while the subtitle says, "Hello. Nice to meet you." It was next to impossible to follow the stories and, in my opinion, both of the movies crowded the boundaries of being soft porn. I was not impressed.

After each movie, Doo-Wayne took me to his favorite little coffeehouse on campus where we would sit on very uncomfortable chairs at a tiny wrought iron table. Doo-Wayne would order an *espresso* for himself and a *café au lait* for me, and then we would spend about an hour discussing the "intellectual merits" of the movie. That meant that I sipped my coffee and listened while Doo-Wayne held forth with the biggest bunch of hooey I had ever heard—all very Bohemian and "with it." In my opinion, Doo-Wayne *deserved* that nasty, black syrup that he was choking down in tiny sips.

On both dates, during the drive back to Paxton, I tried to broach the subject of "just being friends" and keeping our options open by dating other people. It didn't work. Doo-Wayne insisted that we *were* friends, and that friendship was the best basis of all for a lasting, meaningful relationship. He also pointed out that we weren't technically "going steady" so our options were always open. However, where was the need to date other people once you had found your true love? (Such are the dangers of dating a member of the Debate Club.) I wanted to grab him by his ears, shake his head, and scream at him for being so incredibly dense.

As it turned out, Doo-Wayne wasn't one for necking out in the country. I think the dark country roads and the rustling cornfields scared him. Instead, when he brought me home, he would pull into the driveway, turn off the car, and then slide over a little closer to me in the front seat. His eyelids would be at half-mast with one eyebrow lifted, something that he seemed to think was sexy. I thought he just looked like the *espresso* had caught up to him and upset his stomach. He was a Bug Smasher when it came to kissing, but I managed to terrify him with the image of an angry, over-protective father. That kept the mauling in the driveway to a minimum. (Thank God for older sisters!)

Finally, as September started, I decided that the "Doo-Wayne situation" had to be ended for good. School had been back in session for a week, and Doo-Wayne stuck to me like a chewed wad of Dubble-Bubble on the sole of a tennis shoe. People were beginning to gossip and giggle. A couple of my girl-friends had already asked me if he and I were an "item," and if we were, for Heaven's sake, *why?* I wasn't sure exactly *how* I was going to slay this particu-lar dragon but, if I wanted any peace in my life, I was going to *have* to do it. Pulling my determination together, I agreed to go to another movie with Doo-Wayne.

The evening was another boring carbon-copy of the others, and by the time Doo-Wayne brought me home I was no closer to achieving my goal than I had been when we left. When we pulled into the driveway, Doo-Wayne noticed that our family car was gone, and he asked if my parents were home. I told him that Mom and Dad had gone to a retirement party for one of Dad's co-workers at the airbase, and even as I finished saying it I realized that I had goofed-up, big time. His eyes gleamed. Aha! No avenging father on the pre-mises tonight! He started to move in, his lips already all pinched up.

I looked around in a panic and blurted out the first thing that came to my mind, "Let's go for a little walk."

"A walk? Now? Where?"

Okay, it was a dumb idea, but since I had already said it I now seized on it like it was an answer to prayer. "Right here, in the backyard. It's a beautiful evening. Come on." I quickly opened the door on my side of the car and slid out. Doo-Wayne followed me much more slowly. I took his hand and started leading him to the backyard.

Now, most people will think that a walk through the backyard isn't such a big deal and can't consume more than three minutes. Our backyard, however, was almost two acres of land and offered a lot more possibilities.

It *was* a beautiful evening—it was pleasantly cool and a bright half moon sailed high above us. It had been a warm day, and the cool evening air was causing a slight ground fog to rise. Wisps of mist were rising from the ground, drifting and swirling here and there at about knee level. Since we were on the edge of town there was very little background light. We walked slowly, and once our eyes adjusted to the dark we could see more than well enough to nav-igate.

I led Doo-Wayne out to the front edge of the garden and had him look south. On the horizon, you could see the lights of Rantoul and the airbase, ten miles away. I led him deeper into the yard, past the garden and well out into what Dad called the "back forty." About ten feet from the property line we stopped again, and I told Doo-Wayne to look up. He gasped in surprise at the thousands upon thousands of stars that could be seen, and I pointed out some of the better known constellations. After a few minutes, we brought our gaze back to earth and it was then that Doo-Wayne spotted our back fence and, more importantly, what lay beyond our back fence.

"Is that the cemetery over there?" he asked.

"What?"

"Your next door neighbor is the cemetery?"

"Oh. Yes, it is—it's a really neat place." When you grow up next to a cemetery, particularly with a pair of levelheaded parents, you don't harbor much foolishness about spooks. To us, it was almost like an extension of our yard. Mom and Dad had taught us to be respectful of the graves when we were out there, which was often. I had explored it from end to end, I had read the inscriptions on most of the gravestones, and I had learned to ride my bike on its quiet, paved roads.

"Doesn't it bother you to live next to the cemetery?"

"Not at all. Here, let me show you something." I grabbed Doo-Wayne's hand and dragged him the ten feet to the fence. "If you look carefully, over there, do you see that little angel with the broken wing? It's one of my favorite markers."

He peered where I was pointing and said, "Oh, yes, I think I do see it. It's kind of far away, though, isn't it? I've never seen it before."

"Haven't you ever been in the cemetery?"

"Well, I was in there several years ago on Memorial Day. My Boy Scout troop was part of the parade, but I didn't pay much attention to what was around me."

"And that's it?" You've only been out there once?"

In answer, he nodded nervously.

I firmly believe that it was at that moment in time when the Devil gently took my hand, whispered in my ear, and began to lead me through the subsequent ballet of that night. At least, I long ago decided that if I was ever called onto the carpet about those events, that would be my defense—temporary demonic possession.

I looked at Doo-Wayne in wide-eyed innocence and said, "The cemetery is a *wonderful* place! It's beautifully kept up, and it's like a big park with an art gallery included—some of the monuments are incredible." The Devil tugged on my hand, and I added, "Come on! I'll show you!" I was wearing slacks, and with the ease of long practice I climbed over the fence. I took a few steps and turned back to Doo-Wayne with my hand held out. Very slowly, he followed me.

With Doo-Wayne clutching my hand, I led him deeper and deeper into the cemetery. I pointed out sculptured markers, sentimental inscriptions, and interesting epitaphs. He gradually relaxed a little as he realized that we weren't going to be chased by any ghosts or skeletons. I finally got him to the center of the cemetery on a small hill just past the monument to the Unknown Soldier. We always called this area "Monument Hill" because there were a lot of large, imposing markers. Doo-Wayne got so interested in one that he actually let go of my hand as he leaned forward to make out the inscription.

The Devil whispered in my ear. Very quietly, I took a few steps backward and then a few more steps to the side, placing myself behind a neighboring monument. I glanced around. The ground fog was getting a little thicker and now reached about hip high. It produced a *very* interesting effect as it drifted and swirled among the tombstones in the moonlight. With a slight shrug, I headed for home.

A few minutes later, I let myself into the house through the front door. Donna was in the living room, watching a show on TV. She glanced up at me and asked, "So, how was the date with Doo-Wayne?"

I rolled my eyes in answer and said, "It was a Doo-Wayne date. I'm kinda tired. I think I'll just go up to my room and read for awhile."

"Okay. Catch you later."

About twenty minutes later, Donna came upstairs and walked into my room. "Pat? Where's DeWayne?"

"I don't know. I'd assume that he's at home by now."

"I don't think so. His car is still in the driveway, but there's no sign of him anywhere."

"Oh, for Heaven's sake! Do you mean he hasn't gotten back yet?"

"Back from where?"

"Um-m-m-m, I don't know."

"Pat! Where is DeWayne?"

"I told you—I don't know *where* he is at this moment."

Donna took a deep breath and said, "All right, then, where did you leave him?"

I paused for a second, and then said in a small voice, "In the cemetery."

"The cemetery! What were you doing out there?"

"Walking. And a near-sighted chipmunk could've found its way back by now!"

"Are you telling me that you conned DeWayne Smith out into the cemetery at night, and then you just *left* him out there?"

"Well, yeah, that's about what happened."

"Oh, for God's sake, what is the matter with you? Listen, you stay here so there's someone in the house with Raymond. I'll go out and try to find him."

"It's just the cemetery."

"And some people are really scared of cemeteries. We'll be lucky if he hasn't had a heart attack!" She turned on her heel and stormed out of my room. A few minutes later I heard the back door open and close as Donna set out on her rescue mission.

Donna had taken Dad's big flashlight with her, and it didn't take her long to find DeWayne. He was near where I had left him, standing with his back flattened up against a large tombstone and his teeth chattering. She softly "talked him down" and then gently led him out of the cemetery and back to the house. At first he refused to come into the house, but since he was still trembling all over Donna insisted that he come in. She made a cup of strong, sweet tea with milk in it. She then made DeWayne sit down at the table and drink it before he left. From upstairs, I could hear the murmur of her voice as she talked to him while he drank his tea. Finally, I heard the front door open and close, followed by the sound of DeWayne's car when he backed out of the driveway.

Right after he had driven away, I heard the sound of my sister's footsteps as she stomped back through the house, up the stairs, and into my room. I looked up to find her glaring at me with her hands on her hips.

"Patricia Jean! You should be totally ashamed of yourself! What in the world possessed you to do that?"

"I don't know—it just came over me as a way to finally get rid of Doo-Wayne."

"Yeah, well you almost did it permanently. I think he was in shock. You're just damned lucky that Mom and Dad aren't home! They'd ground you for the rest of your life for a stunt like that!"

"You're not going to tell them, are you?"

"I ought to, and it'd serve you right!" She paused and thought for a few moments, and then said in a much softer tone, "No, I won't tell them that you're that much of a rat."

"I guess I should apologize to Doo-Wayne."

"I don't think DeWayne Smith will ever again let you get close enough to him to even try to apologize. The best thing you can do from now on is to just leave him alone."

"That's fine, if he'll leave me alone."

"Trust me, after tonight, he will. Listen, I talked to him while he was downstairs, and I think I managed to smooth this out a little bit."

"What did you say?"

"I pointed out that Mom and Dad were probably right, and you aren't old enough or mature enough to be dating. I agreed that it was a bum stunt, and I *did* apologize for your behavior. The best you can hope for now is that he keeps his mouth shut around school, or you'll never have another date in your life."

"You don't think he'll tell anyone, do you?"

"No, I don't think he will. It would be way too embarrassing for him." Donna sat down on my bed and just looked at me for a minute. Slowly, she started to smile. "Well, it was a truly unique solution to the problem, wasn't it?"

"Yeah, and the best of it was that it worked."

We looked into each other's eyes for a moment with total understanding. That look encompassed boys, dating, necking, teenage social disasters, and all the secrets that can only be shared by sisters. Then we both collapsed in laughter.

'Til Next Time ...

We started this volume by answering a question about how true and accurate our stories are. We would like to close it by answering another question we get asked from time to time: do we believe that things were better in the past, and that people would do well to try to return to that environment?

No, we don't think it's a good idea to try to live in the past. Life is about growing and changing, and in this universe time moves forward and carries all of us along with it. Also, we thoroughly appreciate things like dishwashers, air conditioners in cars, CD's, DVD's, and computerized word processing. We both learned to type on manual Royal typewriters that required the typist to "throw" the carriage at the end of each line, and revisions usually meant retyping the entire document. Trust us—today's tools make a lot of life a lot easier.

We also do not consider the past to be a time of idyllic utopia. There was plenty of stress to deal with while we were growing up. The Cold War was in full swing, and a popular project for a lot of people was the construction of fallout shelters. Isn't that a jolly thought? We are also members of the Vietnam generation, and both of us had friends who never returned and whose names are now on a wall in Washington, DC. On a day-to-day basis, people worked hard and struggled with the same type of personal problems that we do today. In other words, life in the past was simply life, and people dealt with it as they still do.

We do believe, however, that the past is an important part of all of us. It helped shape us into the people we are today, and we need to remember and be thankful for those incidents and influences that formed our lives. We have also found, as is usual with memory, that it is easier and a lot more fun to remember the good experiences. Why not, if it brings a smile or a ray of sunshine into your day?

That is the spirit that motivates us to write these books and share these stories with you. We hope we have brought a smile to your day, and also encouraged you to remember some of your own experiences. One of our readers told us that she keeps her copies of our books on her end table. When her two-year-old has driven her almost to distraction, she will sit down, pick up a book, open it at random and read a story. She says that little "story break" helps her to relax and put things back in perspective. We were delighted.

It is now time for us to close this volume and get to work on our next project. There are still more stories to be told, and we are planning to try our hands at a book of stories for children. So, we need to get busy 'til next time.

Donna's National Honor Society Congratulations Cake[1]

Cake Mix:	Mix cake mix ingredients until smooth.
1 box lemon cake mix	Pour into greased and floured tube pan.
4 eggs	Bake at 350 degrees for 45 to 60 minutes.
1 small box lemon jello	
2/3 c. oil	While cake is cooking, mix glaze ingredients
3/4 c. water	Until smooth. As soon as cake is removed from
1 tsp. Lemon extract	Oven, pour glaze mixture over cake. Let cool.
Glaze:	
1 c. powdered sugar	
1/4 c. lemon juice	

---

1. Page 115, *Beach Party*

Letter to Our Readers

Dear Readers,

Plan a day trip to Paxton, Illinois, or, if your travels carry you along I-57 in central Illinois, make a side trip to visit the new Ford County Historical Museum located in the Paxton Water Tower and Pump House, scheduled for it's Grand Opening July 4th, 2007.

It has been a five-year endeavor for the Ford County Historical Society, in alliance with the Paxton Foundation, to complete this project. It was envisioned to be historically accurate, eye grabbing, professionally orchestrated, and fun. The historical society met their goals.

The exhibits were built by Taylor Studios of Rantoul, Illinois who are the successful creators of exhibits at Starved Rock State Park, Rock Springs Nature center, Geneva History Center, and several other public displays.

Bob Maney, of the Ford County Historical Society said of the museum, "The central theme will be a history of Ford County, including its agriculture, industry, people and work the early settlers did to establish the county.

He also emphasized that the Historical Society will host group visits for school children, clubs and social organizations. Of course any and all individuals or families are welcome.

Pat and I will be at the grand opening on July 4th to autograph and/or sell copies of our books. We are very proud of this new museum and the work and planning that went into its creation.

If you need additional information on time schedules or directions to the museum, you can visit their web site at www.rootsweb/~ilfchs or contact Mr. Maney at phone number 217-379-2031.

If you have enjoyed reading
Backyard Bones
please share information about the book
and your reactions with friends.

To order additional copies call 1-877-288-4737
or
Go online at

www.iUniverse.com
www.bn.com
www.Amazon.com
www.paxtonil.com

It can also be ordered through fine
bookstores everywhere.

If you would like to learn more about the town of
Paxton, Illinois, visit their web site at www.paxtonil.com.

978-0-595-45069-5
0-595-45069-5

www.ingramcontent.com/pod-product-compliance
Lightning Source LLC
Chambersburg PA
CBHW022249290526
45785CB00015B/468